GREEN BEHIND THE EARS

by the same author
The Year of the Cornflake

Faith Addis

Green Behind
the Ears

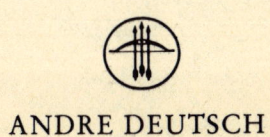
ANDRE DEUTSCH

*To Terry, who showed me a
much better way of doing it.*

First published 1984 by
André Deutsch Limited
105 Great Russell Street London WC1

Printed in Great Britain by
Ebenezer Baylis & Son Ltd
The Trinity Press, Worcester, and London

British Library Cataloguing in Publication Data
Addis, Faith
Green behind the ears.
1. Recreation   2. Vacations
I. Title
790.19'22'0924   GV1203

ISBN 0.223.97659.0

Chapter One

'I SAW YOUR advert in the *Lady*', said a voice at the other end of the phone. 'It sounds so inviting, may I book a night's bed and breakfast for my husband and myself at the end of the month, please?'

'I'm sorry there must be some mistake,' I said. 'We don't advertise in the *Lady*. In fact, we're closed until half term.'

'Half term? Are you a school?'

'No, a guest house, but we only take children.'

'Gosh, what fun!'

Fun? For the past six months (this was September) my husband Brian and I had played host to seventy-nine unaccompanied children. Not all at once, although sometimes it seemed that way, but in batches of up to twenty at a time. They had come in assorted sizes and colours and had one thing in common — they ate. They ate breakfast, elevenses, lunch, tea and supper; and if they got peckish in between meals they ate biscuits, chocolate and apples. When they weren't eating they were riding our ponies and generally enjoying themselves on our seven-acre smallholding in Devon.

'Fun for them,' I acknowledged to the caller, 'but quite tiring for us. What's the date on your *Lady*?'

'1975. Oh dear, that's last year, isn't it? I suppose you couldn't stretch a point as you're empty, could you? We love old houses and it says in this advert that there are panoramic views of the valley.'

So the previous owners had cashed in on the views too. It must have been their ad in the *Lady* as we had only advertised in the *Sunday Times*. It seemed a waste of a good ad to say no, so I said yes. After all, it was only for one night and we needed every penny to see us through to the following holiday season.

'Oh, thank you,' said the caller. 'Shall we be sleeping in a dorm? It's ages since I slept in a dorm.'

1

'No, it's quite civilised,' I reassured her. Or would be to a dung beetle, I added mentally. Thank goodness visual telephones hadn't arrived yet. We exchanged names and addresses and I said I would confirm by post, then we rang off.

I took stock of our quite civilised home and panoramic views. There wasn't an awful lot of view to be had as none of the windows had been cleaned since Easter, and were almost opaque from having withstood the sticky-fingered summer guests.

There had been a fourteen-week drought and windows had been way down the pecking order when it came to water. The rain, when it came, had not been sufficient to fill the reservoir, and we were still being miserly with water in the house, so as to have enough for winter brassicas, leeks, carrots and pansies.

The pansies were Brian's idea. He had read an article in a horticultural trade paper about how to become a millionaire by growing flowers for seed. Money for old rope, he reckoned, and sent away for further details. A representative from a well-known flower-seed firm had called, first to see if our premises were suitable — they were, being south-facing and loamy — then a second visit to check on Brian himself. He was pretty loamy after fourteen weeks without a bath and his pH must have been all right, because the rep said his firm would let Brian grow for them. They sent four ounces of pansy seed and strict instructions about cultivation and harvest.

So, although we had our first million pounds germinating away busily below ground, it would be a full year before harvest and for the time being we were, as usual, broke.

Banks are not too happy to lend on four ounces of pansy seed and we decided that if our bed and breakfast guests lived to tell the tale, we would advertise for a few more out of season. Our accountant was all for it too. He had nearly thrown in the sponge when we sent him our incoming and outgoing figures for the holiday children. It seemed there was rather too much out and not enough in; we had made a loss of 4p per child. 'What did you feed them on — sirloin?' he had written.

And the pigs and ponies had cost a lot more than we had estimated. We had based our costings on John Seymour's self sufficiency book which is frankly inaccurate when it comes to pigs. You can't give them half the recommended rations and hope they will make up the balance on scraps. Not unless you have very superior scraps and our locust-like guests soon put paid to that idea.

The ponies, Monty, Wellington, Noah and Rocky plus a few on loan for the summer had got through some money too. Mainly on shoes which they wore out at an alarming rate.

We had just two weeks in which to make the house look presentable. I'm pig-proud – pigs are so appreciative – but not all that houseproud. I only wish I could drum up the enthusiasm for housework that I have for mucking out. It gets easier as you get older; you can drop the 'I'm not wasting my intellect on domestic drudgery' attitude – an attitude which wastes far more energy than the chores themselves, but of course encroaching old age also means that by the time you've seen to the animals and cleared away the breakfast things you're knackered.

There were twelve bedrooms and four reception rooms to be turned out. Our sixteen-year-old daughter Sara who should have been on tap to halve the workload had skipped off for a holiday to friends in London. Not that she would have been much help. She had suddenly started a 'my parents don't understand me' phase, and was about as useful as a puppy round the house. Her elder brother Marcus was out at work all day: a trainee civil servant in an office so overstaffed that he had time to write a six thousand word article for a motorbike magazine during his first fortnight.

So, with both children otherwise engaged and a husband who had to stay outdoors hewing and sowing and reaping, there was nothing for it but to get started.

Seven bedrooms later I felt I had earned a break, so I invited myself to tea with Ursula, our friend and neighbour. Until quite recently, Ursula had taken in paying guests to eke out her widow's pension and I wanted to bend her ear.

'Stick him on the floor,' Ursula said, indicating Cinnamon, who was curled up in the softest armchair. Cinnamon grumbled the way cairns do, then brightened up as he spotted his girlfriend, Parsley. Parsley is my cavalier, a terrible flirt and the love of Cinnamon's life.

3

Picking my way round a pyramid of packing cases — Ursula was shortly moving to a cottage half a mile away — I subsided into Cinnamon's chair. Ursula handed me a cup of tea. 'You look hot,' she said.

'I'm cleaning up for the bed and breakfasters. We're a bit nervous to tell you the truth. Were you nervous when you started?'

Ursula laughed. 'I was fine when I started and a nervous wreck when I finished.'

'Why? What happened?'

'Well, at first all the guests were great fun — like having one's own friends to stay. Then I tried to economise on advertising and that *was* a mistake. I used one of those national advertising papers — you know, the sort with such small print you need twenty twenty vision to read it. Anyway, this chap came to stay, *not* a gentleman. He actually used his eggshell as an ashtray!'

For some reason, I found the idea of Neanderthal PGs creasingly funny. I pictured them seated round the breakfast table, papers propped on sticky-lidded sauce bottles crushing dog end after dog end into their eggshells.

'I don't suppose all their readers behave like that, Ursula.'

'No, I was just unlucky. But if you're going in for bed and breakfast, I should stick to the glossies if I were you.'

'That reminds me, have you got any spare sheets and things for sale, or did you get rid of your surplus stuff when you stopped taking guests?'

'I've some linen, and I've decided to sell one of my freezers. I won't have room for two in the cottage.'

'We'll buy it. And all the linen too please.'

Our own freezer was bursting at the seams with blackberries and runner beans, over 100 lb of each, and more to come if anyone could find time to pick them.

Ursula's sheets and pillowcases were real linen, crispy and stiff from proper laundering. 'Brian'll love these,' I said, fingering the edges. 'He'd have liked to have been high-born and had elegant houses and flunkeys and things.'

Ursula was high-born, but her people had been poor. Her father had had to sell some of his hunters to make ends meet.

4

'They'll probably bring you out in a rash,' Ursula said, shattering my lavender-sachet illusion. 'You sleep in the raw, don't you?'

Sometimes I think country houses must be bugged. You can't sneeze without someone from a distant village phoning up with offers of hot toddy. When Marcus got his first job in Exeter, twenty-eight miles away, he phoned home to tell us and before he arrived home, we had a phone call, saying wasn't it good about Marcus's job.

I said I'd better be getting back to the spring-cleaning.

'You sound enthusiastic I must say. Can't Sara give you a hand?'

'She's in London. She's got some crazy notion of enrolling at a polytechnic, and retaking her O levels.'

'Where would she stay?'

'With friends of ours. She seems to think she can get a grant to pay for her keep. She's fed up with us.'

'Faith dear, you and Brian are fatheads,' said Ursula kindly. 'Let her go, stop all this gasket blowing over a few failed O levels. Fix up her London accommodation yourselves, help her pack and send her off with your blessings.'

'At sixteen? Alone in London?'

'Oh, for goodness sake! She'll be with your friends, won't she? And anyway, Sara's been capable of looking after herself since she cut her teeth.'

Cheered by Ursula's Earl Grey and advice, I staggered home with half a hundredweight of up-market bedding. We *would* have to let Sara go, we *were* fatheads. After all, I argued with myself, mares let their foals go, bitches let their pups, cats let . . . oh *hell*. I'd forgotten to tell Brian that Small was in one of the bedrooms. She was being starved prior to her spaying operation which was booked for today.

I dumped the sheets on the kitchen table and went upstairs. Small's room was empty. From the window, I could see Brian pulling up pea haulm in the garden.

'Where's Small?' I called. Brian straightened up and rubbed his back.

'Small,' I repeated.

He parked his spade and started back across the garden to

the house. I could see a balloon with 'tea' coming out of his head, so I went downstairs and put the kettle on. If ever Brian had to do one of those psychologist's word association tests he would say 'tea' if they said 'wife'.

Small was at the vet's, he informed me smugly. *He* had remembered even if some people were too busy socialising to care about their responsibilities. He liked the sheets, embossed now with tiny paw prints from Small's kittens, Humphrey and Smallest.

'When can we collect her?' I asked, dropping bits of chocolate digestive into Honey's mouth.

'Don't do that, she'll get fat. Tomorrow morning, stitches out in a week.'

'She'll never get fat.' Honey was a ten-year-old whippet cross, thin as Brian and beginning to get crotchety in damp weather.

The kittens pelted round and round the kitchen, stopping every so often to kill a piece of string attached to a ferocious cottonreel.

'It's time we found homes for them.' Brian has nightmares about animals. He likes them in manageable numbers like one. To get him off that theme, I told him what Ursula had said about letting Sara go to London.

As a result of this, and other discussions with Sara's prospective landlord, her immediate future was decided. Within the next couple of weeks, her red-spotted handkerchief was slung over the traditional stick and off she sallied, feeling, we suspected, a lot less jaunty than she would have us believe. Little did we imagine as we waved the train goodbye that the next time we saw her would be in unthinkably ghastly circumstances.

The first bed and breakfasters — the ones that had come via the *Lady* — were really nice, so friendly that soon we were on Christian name terms and wondering why we were bothering with unaccompanied children. Their overnight stay stretched into several days; they took their evening meals with us after which we would chat over coffee until bedtime. We were sorry to see them go and kept in touch with Christmas cards for some time.

The next couple could not have been a greater contrast. The trouble was, they quarrelled all the time, and the husband always came off worse. Brian and I row a lot, usually over missing shirt buttons or hoof prints, but our rows usually end in a draw and are held behind closed doors. This couple would hold post-mortems over games of bridge they had played, sometimes going back into pre-history for ammunition. 'What about that ridiculous two hearts opening you made at the Postlethwaites' in July,' she would say. (*July* for God's sake!) And he, poor worm, instead of laughing it off as water under the bridge, would rise to the bait and remember the strong spades *she* had been holding when he made his two hearts bid. And so it would go on. Luckily for them, they left before I got round to putting ground glass in their scrambled eggs.

Our third couple sounded fine over the phone. Both in their eighties, he a retired Brigadier or Admiral or something martial; she straight out of Kipling – honest Injun. Easy, we thought, and started planning appetising light supper snacks for them, full of eggs and butter but without nuts so as not to tax their dentures.

They arrived, fit as a pair of racing greyhounds, and said they would rather eat *en famille*. On their first evening, they joined us in roast pork, roast potatoes, roast parsnips and runner beans all awash with gravy made from the pork dripping and juices. For pudding we had Spotted Dick with syrup and cream and then some runny Brie with crackers. I would not normally serve such an unbalanced meal to guests but, having thought they would eat separately, had cooked our usual trying-to-put-weight-on-Brian type of meal. We had all lost weight during the summer and Brian in particular could have modelled for an Oxfam poster.

Dinner over, the old couple, who should have been having coronaries after all that pork, accepted Brian's offer of a drink with their coffee. Mrs Ex-Warrior favoured Crème de Menthe while the old campaigner stuck to Glenfiddich. Like a leech. Half a bottle oiled his memory no end. He had been in his fifties during the last war and had directed his regiment or fleet quite cannily from Whitehall.

'Grand chaps, grand chaps; never let you down, eh?' His lady nodded agreement. I wondered if Brian would show them the hole in his bottom, a memento of basic training days when a fellow conscript had accidentally fired a rifle he was cleaning. Grand chaps they may have been but not particularly careful where they put their bullets.

But Brian was in his cups too and didn't contribute much to the conversation. The only reason we have spirits in the house is because we don't much like the taste and the Christmas hoard gathers dust until someone else drinks it. It was two o'clock when we finally winched ourselves to bed and a few seconds later the alarm clock was bossily informing us it was seven o'clock and time to get cracking.

Our guests had fruit juice, ham and eggs, and toast and honey for breakfast. We had aspirins. Then they drove off to Lyme Regis where they planned to have a round of golf before lunch and a cliff-top walk after.

Brian milked the cow and I fed the animals and let the ducks and chickens out. We met back in the kitchen and risked a conversation – a verbless monosyllabic exchange – over a pot of tea.

But the aspirins did their work and the day flew by. Soon our perky pair were back, irons poised, ready for a second innings. Lamb chops, apple pie and the rest of the Brie disappeared, then we had the First World War with brandy.

Next morning we waved them goodbye, then swore a solemn oath never to have adult guests again. However tiresome children are, you can always pack them off to bed, and if they object you can sing them a lullaby or give them a thick ear, depending how you feel. You cannot, unless you're running a different sort of establishment, put adults to bed. But it had been an interesting experiment. Expensive, too.

Chapter Two

WITH WINTER round the corner, it was time to sell all but the nucleus of our livestock. In a normal year, we should probably have overwintered most of the animals, and even added a few as we had plenty of stabling and seven acres of goodish grass, but the long summer drought had put paid to the grass and hay was virtually unobtainable.

All four goats were the first to go. One of the nannies had twin billy kids which she refused to suckle, and we hadn't bothered to mate the other. Most goat owners will go overboard about the virtues of goats, but we found them noisy, unintelligent animals and quite filthy compared to pigs. They would wet and mess over every inch of their pen, including their feeding area, and after a year of cleaning up after them, we were glad of the extra hours we gained by selling them.

Bambi, our old Jersey house-cow was the next to go. Unhappily, not to a new owner, but to the great permanent pasture in the sky. She had been much older than we realised when we'd bought her the previous year and had failed to come into season after the birth of her last calf. Then her milk dried up, and her calf had to be weaned. We simply could not afford to keep a barren, milkless cow so, cursing the drought and hating ourselves, we had her shot. Then we sold her calf and mourned the two of them. It was a desolate time.

The sows Phyll and Rosie each had a litter of weaners ready to sell. Some were Large White by a nominated A1 boar, and some were pure bred Gloucester Old Spots which Rosie had fostered. All the piglets had been outdoor reared and milk fed, and were a classy looking bunch. We put an advert in *Farmers' Weekly* and were overwhelmed with phone calls from prospective customers wanting naturally-reared breeding stock.

We kept Rose Hip, the best of the Gloucester Old Spot

9

gilts, and spent a happy weekend meeting pig lovers who came to buy the rest. They were all smallholders like ourselves, and we were confident that our precious weaners would have good homes. All except one.

The best Gloucester Old Spot boar had been reserved over the phone by a man called Erskine from Lincolnshire. He drove down with his family, and when they got out of their car my heart sank. He was a swarthy unshaven man with a pushed back cap, two hairy, villainous looking six-foot sons and a wife who should have been in a tent telling fortunes.

'Oh, *no*,' I breathed. 'Not *dealers*.'

Brian looked uneasy. 'Hope they don't haggle,' he said.

The man picked up the nine-week-old piglet in one massive hand and examined it. 'He'll do,' he said, and peeled fifty pounds off a fat wad of tenners. We offered them all a cup of tea after their long journey, and to my dismay they accepted, and came indoors. Everyone was rather ill at ease. Brian handed round mugs of tea, and I started to copy out the piglet's pedigree form but, apprehensive of the raping and pillaging I was sure was going to break out any minute, I kept making mistakes. Marcus was home as it was Saturday, and offered to do it. He is rather a dab hand at lettering and can even do italic script if he concentrates. I doubted whether any of them could read or write, but thankfully let him take over anyway. Eventually they drained their mugs and filed out, the sons ducking their heads under the doorway.

We lifted the piglet into their small trailer and piled plenty of straw round him. He looked very frightened and forlorn. The man tied a tarpaulin over the trailer and knotted it firmly. 'Proper job,' he said and off they drove.

What with being so busy selling the rest of the weaners, the incident of the Lincolnshire gipsies was not uppermost in my mind when I answered the phone at six o'clock on Sunday evening.

'Edward's eaten a good tea,' said a woman's voice. 'And he's gone for a walk with Roger.'

'Edward?' I said stupidly. 'Roger?' I have a good memory for names as a rule, but couldn't for the life of me recall an Edward or a Roger.

'He didn't travel well,' the woman went on. 'He was sick so we gave him some glucose when we got home like you told us to.'

'Golly!' I said, (meaning golly, someone has actually *listened* to my advice, and just wait until I tell Brian). I am always handing out homilies, mostly of a herbal nature, and usually people just glaze over and go deaf. 'Well, I'm glad the glucose did the trick, Mrs 'um?'

'Erskine,' said the woman.

'Erskine?' It *couldn't* be. 'From Lincolnshire?'

'Well, we haven't moved since yesterday.' Mrs Erskine understandably sounded a little sharp.

'I'm so sorry, Mrs Erskine, we've been selling piglets all weekend, and I was a bit muddled. I didn't know you'd called the pig Roger.'

'Edward. Roger's our son. We bought him the pig for his birthday. I just thought you'd like to know how he was – you looked proper upset when Edward was in the trailer.'

I could hardly tell her why I looked upset, so I said nothing. She went on, 'We gave him a warm mash at breakfast and he slept right through till tea. Then he ate a good tea so Roger's taken him for a bit of a walk on a lead.'

Still I said nothing. I could picture Roger in a stocking mask brandishing a sawn-off shotgun but by no stretch of the imagination could I see him walking Edward on a lead.

'Oh, and another thing,' said Mrs Erskine.

'Yes?' Go on, tell me your other son's been offered the male lead in Swan Lake.

'That pedigree form. There's a mistake in the sire line. Winterwood Prince the Second can't be Edward's father and grandfather. According to the National Pig Breeders' herd register Bella was put to Winterwood Prince the First. Her previous service was to Gerald of Tuscany.'

'I'll check the pedigree forms, Mrs Erskine, and send you another copy. Sorry about that.'

'Thanks. You see Roger wants to show Edward and later on we'll probably get him an unrelated gilt. Don't bother with that fancy writing, just print it nice and plain.'

'Yes, I will. I'm sorry.'

Truly sorry. One hundred per cent sorry.

In October Brian went away for a week to visit smallholding friends in North Wales. He put up a token show of resistance but Marcus backed me up when I said we could easily manage on our own. Easier as it turned out, because Marcus collected fish and chips on his way home from work each evening and I did no cooking at all. Or housework. Brian phoned home once or twice to say yes, he was enjoying himself; yes, they loved Humphrey (our friends had given us Small the previous year, so we felt we were quits by giving them her kitten, Humphrey), and how were we managing? Nicely we said, not mentioning the fish and chips.

Then one evening Parsley had puppies. I was caught on the hop with nothing prepared for her confinement which was six days early. She had been a little restless and kept asking to be let out. Marcus and I, deep in books in front of a huge log fire as it was a frosty night, took it in turns to let her out and then in again.

At about ten o'clock Marcus said, 'She's been outside a long time, I'll get her in,' and the next thing I knew was that my book was being snatched away and a black, slug-cold object thrust into my hands.

'Quick – *please* be quick!' Marcus, usually so unflappable pulled me out of the armchair and ran back outside shouting, 'She's having them all over the rockery – hurry!'

I put my brain into gear. The creature in my hands was moving, *ergo* there must be some hope. Tucking the puppy inside my polo-necked jumper, I ran to the kitchen, took a towel from the rail in front of the Rayburn and crumpled it into the bottom oven. I kissed the cold stumpy face and with a hurried 'good luck, mate,' thrust the puppy into the half-open oven and went out to look for Parsley.

It was cold outside and the garden was white with frost. An oblong of light from the kitchen window illuminated Marcus kneeling on the boulders of the rockery holding something in his cupped hands.

'Take it,' he said in rather a choky voice. 'It's all slimy.'

12

It was slimy, much warmer than the first puppy and its umbilical cord was still thick and fleshy. I posted it down my polo neck and it wriggled vigorously.

'Good,' I said. 'It's only a few minutes old. Can you see Parsley?'

'I think she's gone under the chalet,' said Marcus.

Borrowing a Covent Garden porter expression, I hurtled down the frozen steps and just missed Parsley's tail disappearing under the chalet which stood on nine-inch sleepers.

'I'll see if I can reach her,' Marcus said, and inched himself head first between the sleepers. His shoulders stuck and he tried again feet first. Boys' hips are just the right size for rescuing spaniels under chalets, and soon he had Parsley captive between slippered feet. He wriggled backwards.

'Got her,' I said, grabbing a handful of scruff. She was covered in cobwebs, blood and earth, and smelt like a cave.

'You take the torch,' said Marcus, 'and give me Parsley to carry.'

Back in the warm kitchen Honey and Small were peering into the Rayburn, from where a very cross small voice was demanding to see someone in authority. He sounded like a tiny chainsaw.

'He's alive!'

'Fantastic,' said Marcus. 'Shall I go and see if there are any more outside?'

'There won't be,' I said, popping number two into the oven to meet his brother. 'Not unless this was one of twins.'

'I think I will, just to be on the safe side.' Marcus put Parsley in her basket and went out again. Parsley tried to follow him.

'Oh, no you don't, madam,' I said, spreading some newspapers over her blanket and scooping her back to bed. 'We don't want any more of that natural childbirth nonsense in this weather.' I held her cobwebby face and gently cheered her on as she gave birth to her third son. She looked at it for a moment, puzzled, then the penny dropped and she began to lick it clean.

Marcus reappeared carrying four slippers just as I was lifting the afterbirth on to a newspaper.

13

'I wish Brian was here,' he said feelingly. 'Can I phone him while you're, er, doing whatever it is you're doing?' He looked fixedly at the wall.

'Yes, do. Only put the kettle on first and a small saucepan of water. May as well finish the job text-book fashion.'

'Why *do* people want boiling water for births? Don't tell me if it's too clinical.'

I laughed. 'The kettle's for tea and hot-water bottles and the saucepan's for boiling up scissors and string. The string's for tying their cords if anything goes wrong and . . .'

'Stop, that's enough. Gosh, I'm glad I was found under a gooseberry bush.' And off he went to phone Brian.

I burned the soiled newspapers, washed my hands and made a pot of tea. Parsley, unaware of the trouble she had caused had gone to sleep with puppy number three already tugging at a teat. So far so good, I thought, peeping into the Rayburn to check on the oven-ready brothers. They looked fine, a bit crusty with dried blood but seemingly none the worse for their traumatic entry into the world.

Marcus came back grinning broadly. 'I told Brian he was the grandfather of triplets – nearly had him going for a moment – and he sends love and says keep up the good work in the Lindo Wing. I didn't tell him about them being in the oven.'

'Why not?'

'Well, you know what he's like. It would put him off rice puddings for life. Do you remember how he went mad that time I dried my socks in the Rayburn?'

'Talking of being squeamish, Marcus, you've been marvellous tonight. I didn't think you could stomach gore.'

'I can't,' said Marcus firmly. 'I'm only available in emergencies. Can I name my two pups?'

'M'm, good idea.'

'Kickstart and Revvup?'

Not such a good idea. Oh well, it was only until they went to their new owners. (In the event, Kickstart and Revvup were bought together and renamed Byron and Boswell.)

'When you've had your tea,' I said, 'you'd better go and bath. You look an absolute sight.'

'You don't look exactly like the front cover of *Vogue* yourself,' Marcus said.

14

But I didn't mind. I was in my element. Some people get their kicks from winning the Derby or opening the batting for Somerset, but ever since I assisted at a hippo birth at the London Zoo and had the beautiful ugly baby named after me, I've been a birth addict. Sitting up half the night playing midwife was going to be right up my street.

And so it was. Marcus went to bed at one o'clock, after making me promise to call him if I needed a hand. Everything went well, and at three o'clock, Parsley looking like a deflated balloon, produced her fifth and final puppy. She cleaned it, aimed it towards a vacant teat and sighed contentedly.

'You're the cleverest cavalier in the world,' I told her. She agreed, and said was I going to drink *all* that Ovaltine or could the cleverest cavalier in the world have some? I put some glucose and a raw egg into her share of the Ovaltine, and held the dish for her as she half sat up and drank thirstily.

With a last look at the basketful of squirming puppies, I tore myself away and staggered up to bed, satisfied with a job well done and happy too that Parsley had just presented us with the wherewithal to knock £250 off the overdraft.

Brian came home the next day and walked straight past the teapot to see Parsley. For someone who claims to be unsentimental about animals, he put up a remarkably good show: '*Five*. Who's a clever girl then? Which one is Kickstart? Hullo Kickstart, I hear you had a near miss on that nasty rockery. All better now, are you? That's good. And who are you?' He picked up one of the puppies.

'That one hasn't got a name yet, we left it for you to choose. Marcus named Kickstart and Revvup, and I called the next two Nutmeg and Caraway, so it's your turn. She's the only girl.'

'Nutmeg and Caraway. Does that mean you've been cleaning out the larder?' asked Brian hopefully.

'No.'

'Been cooking?'

'No.'

Brian put the puppy back in the basket. Parsley inspected her for germs – she had after all been out of the nest for all of ten seconds.

15

'She's like you, isn't she, Parsley?' Brian said. 'Same markings across the shoulders. I'll call her Clover.'

'Clover – that's nice. After Marcus's two, I was afraid you'd go in for something like Spanner. How was Snowdonia?'

'All right, except for the Welsh. God, they're a dreary lot up there. And the *climate*. There was a snow warning before I left. I don't know how Rob and Ellie can stand it.'

'We've had a frost,' I said.

'Our frosts would be heatwaves up there. What's for dinner?'

'Chops.'

'Good. I'm starving. I would have bought fish and chips on the way home to save you cooking, but it was too early.'

'I'll make some tea,' I said, whizzing to the sink before my guilty face gave the game away. It was nice having him home again, and chops would be a treat after six days of fish and chips.

Brian's visit to our friends in Wales had whetted his appetite for adult company. We had now lived in Devon for a year and had not had time to get to know many people outside our immediate neighbourhood. The 1976 drought had been a good ice-breaker with everyone queuing at the village standpipes or filling churns at the river, but conversation tends to be limited when you're surrounded by tractors ticking over.

One day we had a dinner invitation from a family who farmed fifteen acres a couple of miles away. 'We're going to the Hornabrooks tonight,' we told Ursula, who had dropped in for coffee and found us dredging around in the wardrobe for something halfway decent to wear.

She said, 'Oh, you'll like them. Jim's in oil.' She made him sound like a sardine. 'And Shirley's a marvel. She runs the place on her own when he's away. I think she must have been a model before she married, she's always so elegant. And the children are a credit to them – so intelligent.'

Brian and I looked at each other in horror. Whatever would we find to talk about? Jim was in oil, Brian was in earth; Shirley looked like a model, I like a scarecrow. Their children would be quiet, obedient and allergic to pop music. Ours were not.

We had a marvellous evening. The Paragons were very nice people. The oil that Jim was in was the sort that lives under the earth's crust and it was Jim's job to tell the Government where it was. He said he did it by stabbing a pin into a map of the North Sea. Shirley cooked a mouth-watering meal, that I knew boded ill for me. (Why can't we have home-made soup and profiteroles like the Hornabrooks?), and was as elegant as Ursula had intimated. She was the sort of person who could look smart in a dog blanket, and to this day I don't know how she keeps her nails so nice after a day pulling parsnips.

The children, Patricia and Andrew, were that contradiction in terms, pleasant teenagers. They disappeared after dinner and washed up without being asked or bribed. What a super family, I thought as we went through to the sitting room for coffee. Brian and I homed in on the bookshelves and browsed happily for a while before being startled by the sight of Jim's legs disappearing through a hole in the ceiling. We had been too engrossed in the books to notice that there was a ladder in the room.

'Phew,' I said. 'I thought it was the elderflower wine.'

'Wine?' said Shirley. 'Oh, you mean the ladder. Sorry, I should have explained. Jim took the stairs away.'

'Why?'

'Why?' repeated Shirley thoughtfully. She turned to Jim who was descending carefully with a fresh bottle of home-made wine. 'Why did you take the stairs away, Jim?'

'I'm going to turn them round,' said Jim.

'That's right. He's going to turn them round. Trouble is, he's only home at weekends and there hasn't been time. He's been building a new goat house and an extension on to the cow pens.'

'How long have you been without stairs?' I asked.

'About six months. I'm so used to the ladder now, I forget what it used to be like.'

'Don't you find it a nuisance?'

'Yes. Especially at night. You should see me going up in a nightie and dressing-gown — I have to make two trips to get

17

everything up in one piece. Book, cigarettes and matches first, then down again to switch out the light and carry my cocoa up. But it's not nearly as bad as the time he took the roof off.'

Jim, it seemed, was one of nature's Starters. After concentrated brainwork all the week there was nothing he liked better than to come home and start a new building project. In the twelve years they had been in the house, he had removed walls, doors and the roof. He had taken out windows and put them back in different places. He had dug a swimming pool in the garden. The projects nearly always were finished in the end, and Shirley had added patience to all her other virtues.

Learning how Shirley and Jim managed their smallholding – how they bred peacocks and geese, kept bees and milked goats to name but about a quarter of their activities – made us think about running our own seven acres efficiently instead of haphazardly. So far we had run the place solely for the child guests, but there was no reason why the stock should not be profitable in its own right. Why, for instance, hadn't we thought of breeding New Zealand White rabbits instead of Flopsy Bunny crossbreds? A rabbit is a rabbit to a child, but a good 'converter' is money to the breeder. And what about multi-suckling a house cow, so that there would be two or three calves to sell each year instead of one?

Talking shop with fellow enthusiasts is always exhilarating, and when the enthusiasts have a cosy, book-lined room – with or without a ladder – it makes you wish you could do this sort of thing more often.

'A smallholders' club,' I mused aloud. 'Somewhere where people like us could meet regularly.'

Luckily for us several kindred spirits in Devon and Somerset were thinking along the same lines and fate was shortly going to shove its oar in and bring us together.

It was well after midnight before we found ourselves walking back, as steadily as the elderflower wine permitted.

'Super evening, wasn't it?'

'M'm. Nice family. Good to see a houseful of books again.'

'How about that ladder? Jim's a genuine eccentric boffin, isn't he?'

'Well, nobody's perfect,' Brian said, loyal to his fellow do-it-yourselfer.

'Why is it that you men can get away with not finishing things? If I had half a baby or cooked half a meal, you wouldn't say "nobody's perfect".'

'Talking of meals, why can't we have gazpacho and profiteroles?'

'I can't even pronounce them, let alone cook them.'

I knew now how the expression 'She's my best friend, and I hate her' originated.

Chapter Three

'YOU GOING hunting?' Tony asked, removing his farrier's apron. I took Wellington to the gate, slipped his head collar off and turned him out into the field where the other ponies were already grinding their new shoes into the precious grass.

'Don't you have to be rich to hunt?' I said, playing for time.

'Ten bob, cubbing round here.'

'I haven't any clothes.'

'Well, that should liven things up. Bit painful though, going through the brambles.'

'Save the razor-sharp wit for Brian, please,' I said. 'He'll laugh at all your funnies today because he's got a favour to ask.'

'You can't pay for the shoeing?' Tony hazarded.

'We can. We sold some weaners.'

'What's the favour, then?'

'Brian wants you to help him layer a hedge.'

'That's not a favour. I enjoy hedging. Makes a change from breaking my back shoeing Rocky.' Rocky, the Shetland, had such small feet that Tony always complained he felt more like a watchmaker than a farrier.

Over mugs of tea Brian and Tony fixed a date for the hedging, then Tony returned to hunting.

'Who will you ride – Monty and Wellington?' he said.

'*If* we go I'll walk,' Brian said firmly. He is not at home on horseback, never having quite got the hang of steering or acceleration.

'And I'll take Noah,' I said. 'If I'm going to fall off, I'd rather fall off a 12.2 than a 14.2.'

'Noah's not hunted before,' Tony said dubiously. 'You'd better get him a dropped noseband, you'll never hold him in a snaffle.'

'Hang on,' interrupted Brian. 'This sounds like the thin end

20

of the wedge. It'll end up with hunting regalia for us and masses of new tack for the ponies.'

'One noseband hardly constitutes masses of tack,' I said. 'Anyway, I think we should go. We don't know if we approve of it until we try it.'

'It's not a question of approving,' said Tony, who was whipper-in for his local hunt. 'You keep poultry, your neighbour has a poultry farm. You've got to protect your stock. It's all very well for the anti-hunt loonies to bleat about cruelty, but you bet your boots, if foxes looked like rats they wouldn't have a fan club.'

'You think the antis get steamed up because foxes look appealing?'

'Yes, I do. And *I* don't find foxes appealing, any more than you will when you find your poultry massacred one morning.'

Coincidentally, soon after Tony's prediction, Ursula brought news of a blood bath. Our poultry farmer neighbour, Mrs Edwards, had lost a whole pen of ducks one night and had called in the hunt.

'They're meeting in the village on Saturday,' Ursula said. 'Will you be riding or going on foot?'

'I'm going on Noah.' There. The die was cast.

'You'll never stop him in a snaffle,' said Ursula.

'Have you been talking to Tony?' I said suspiciously.

'No. But you're as green as Noah and with that Exmoor neck on him you'll need brakes. I suggest a Pelham.'

'I'm afraid the exchequer won't run to a Pelham, Ursula.' I could just imagine Brian's reaction if I spent fourteen pounds on a bit for a pony. 'I'll get a dropped noseband; Tony said that would be OK.'

'Is Brian going?'

'Yes. On foot.'

'Oh good, we can go together.'

The weather on the day of the meet was perfect. A cloudless blue sky, a light frost, and air so pure and cold it made your fillings ache. It isn't done to wear a woolly balaclava for hunting and my ears tingled as Noah and I hacked quietly to the village. Noah was slightly disconcerted by his new noseband and kept trying to rub it off on his knee but when he saw the

21

other horses and the hounds he forgot his discomfort.

The hounds thronged in and out of the horses' legs, and let themselves be petted by onlookers. Noah behaved beautifully, hardly fidgeting at all as we waited for the kick off. Then the huntsman blew his horn and hounds moved off. It had been my intention, as befits a novice, to stay quietly at the back but Noah thought it would be more fun at the front. Thanks to the dropped noseband, we were able to compromise and charged up the hill to the first draw somewhere in the middle of the bunch.

By the time the Master had got everyone arranged round the edge of the covert, Noah had decided that hunting was wonderful and was in a sweat with excitement. Every time he heard the horn, he trembled and gathered himself for action.

Then it happened. A huge fox loped out of the bushes and headed *straight towards us*!

'Hoy,' I shouted, but my voice seemed to have gone wrong and only a small gurgle emerged. The fox passed us not three feet away and clambered up a bank. Noah started dancing round in circles, so I thought it might take some of the steam out of him if I rode over to tell the huntsman which way the fox had gone. Noah needed no bidding, and tore across the field at an unasked for gallop, which was embarrassing as everyone else had calm experienced mounts which did as they were told.

'The fox,' I gasped, pulling up next to the huntsman. 'Gone that way.' I had a vague recollection, culled from Jorrocks, that you're supposed to point with your hat, but with Noah being so frisky, I couldn't spare a hand.

'Which fox?' said the huntsman, mounted on a creature the size of Everest.

'What do you mean — which fox? *The* fox of course.'

'My hounds,' said the huntsman politely, 'are on another scent.' And he rode off.

What *could* he mean, another scent? Buffalo? Chanel No. 5? I spotted Brian in the distance chatting to Ursula, and rode over.

'How's he behaving?' Ursula asked, running a hand down Noah's neck. 'He's rather hot.'

22

'He's loving it. And guess what?'

'What?'

'I've seen the fox.'

'A fox,' Ursula corrected. Grief! She was talking the same double dutch at the huntsman.

'We've seen two,' Brian contributed, looking as puzzled as I felt. 'The dogs took no notice.'

'Hounds,' said Ursula. 'No, they're not allowed to follow different lines. At this time of year the youngsters are being taught to hunt as a pack. Do get back to the others, Faith, or you'll miss a run. We'll go round by road.'

I rode back towards the hounds who were by now barking like mad, or giving tongue as we cognoscente have to say. The horn sounded, a whip cracked and suddenly Noah's excitement flowed up my back and prickled my scalp. The dropped noseband could have been made of cobwebs for all the effect it had. Noah took a firm hold of his bit and charged with a group of about twelve horses across a field, through some scratchy bushes, under trees, over a bank and across another field. Someone shouted 'Mind your knee!' but I had my eyes shut and didn't take much notice. Noah galloped on, stopping eventually when he ran out of breath.

Quite a lot of foot followers had driven round to the new venue, among them Ursula and Brian. I slid off Noah, who was blowing like a train and loosened his girths. 'Hi,' I said nonchalantly, as if I hunted three times a week.

'You're covered in blood,' said Brian. 'Where have you been?'

I didn't like to tell them I had my eyes shut, so I said, 'Over there,' and waved vaguely in the direction of the first draw.

'There's a dangerous piece of corrugated iron in that bank,' Ursula said. 'One or two people caught their knees on it.'

'I think it got me on the neck,' I said. 'Their knee height is about my head height.'

'You should have gone on Monty, shouldn't she, Ursula?' Brian said.

Ursula looked at the scratch on my neck. 'M'm, could have been nasty,' she admitted. 'Your carotid artery is in there somewhere.'

23

'Never mind my war wounds, how did you know the hounds would end up here?'

'Ursula knows,' Brian said. 'She says they always run this way.'

Curiouser and curiouser. Were we really attending a hunt where hounds ignored foxes and runs were preordained? It looked like it. In the three hours that followed, I saw no fewer than seven foxes twirling their canes under the very noses of the young hounds who, far from learning to hunt in a pack, were making quite individual arrangements. Two were having an early lunch off someone's dropped cheese sandwiches while some others were quietly copulating under a hedge. The rest had scattered — presumably to avoid the attentions of the whipper-in who was a cert for an early heart attack. He seemed to think it was a hound called Waitress who was responsible for the anarchy, and kept cracking his whip and shouting *Waitress* like some demented customer in a restaurant.

I was aching with bottled-up laughter and wished like mad that Sara was there. Every so often Brian and I compared notes in passing. Ursula went home at lunch time and Brian joined up with some other friends from the village who were having a splinter group hunt with a couple of friendly hounds who had followed them.

Halfway through the afternoon after several more abortive chases the Master decided to call it a day, and blew his horn to tell the hounds it was time to go home. It took quite a while to get them rounded up, but eventually they were all in the horse box, then, before the driver could get the ramp up, they all streamed out again and disappeared into some woods. By this time, Brian and I had joined forces again, so we sat on a grass verge where we had a good view of the entertainment.

'I bet it was Waitress,' I giggled, wiping my eyes on Brian's hanky.

'Mine were called Willing and Wanting,' Brian said, 'by Dolittle.'

'Not really?'

'No, not Dolittle — I made that up. But I think they were called Willing and Wanting.'

We loosened Noah's girths and walked him home, stopping

24

every so often to give him bites of our Marmite sandwiches, which we had forgotten to eat. We clattered into the yard still giggling, and after seeing to Noah's comforts, went indoors for a cup of tea. Hunting, we decided, seemed a harmless enough pastime, especially if Waitress was playing.

Chapter Four

'IM GOING TO BE late home from work tonight,' Marcus said, one grey rainy morning. 'We've got an inter-departmental skittles match. I won't be back until about ten o'clock.'

'Shall I keep some dinner for you or will you get something out?' I said.

'I'll get a snack at the club, but I'd like a proper meal when I get back.' Marcus sometimes went with his colleagues to a civil service social club in Exeter near where he worked in a local government office.

It rained solidly all day, the rain giving way to sleet as the afternoon grew dark. I phoned Marcus at the office. 'Don't come home on your motorbike if this weather keeps up,' I said. 'Get a train and we'll pick you up at Honiton.'

'Thanks, I will. I don't fancy a thirty mile drive in this.'

Brian and I ate our supper and put Marcus's in the oven to keep warm. I fed the dogs and made Parsley go outside for ten minutes. Not as easy as it sounds as she was so besotted with her five puppies she couldn't bear to leave them for a second. Kickstart was her favourite; he must have been the most washed infant in England, and the best fed. He gained weight at an almost visible rate, and had shoulders on him like an Aberdeen Angus. The others — all Blenheims like Parsley — were just as fat but slightly smaller. They were the biggest time wasters imaginable; even Brian couldn't resist stopping to chat to them every time he passed their basket, and as for me, well I was nearly as bad as Parsley.

Ten o'clock came, but Marcus didn't phone. By eleven o'clock we were getting uneasy. Some time after midnight there was a knock on the door. A fair-haired policeman looking not much older than Marcus came straight to the point for which we were grateful.

He was in intensive care in Exeter Hospital. He was unconscious; the extent of his injuries not known.

Brian whispered 'How?' but I didn't hear the policeman's reply, because the kitchen walls were bulging in and out in a most extraordinary fashion — like a distorting mirror. Young Mercury departed and Brian got the car out.

Our Transit van was in dock having a major face-lift and we had bought a small green vehicle of indeterminate breed for £35 to tide us over. It was a good car for the money, but it had one or two drawbacks, like needing a drink every ten miles and having a top speed of 30 mph. So we had plenty of time in the thirty mile drive to Exeter to imagine Marcus crippled/in the morgue/in the cemetery. Brian smoked and smoked and I stuffed my gloves between my teeth to stop them rattling.

The Sister took one look at us and ordered tea. 'I don't take sugar,' I said.

'You do here,' she said firmly, and stood over us as we drank the syrupy liquid and ate sugar-coated biscuits.

When I saw Marcus, I thought he was dead. They had cut off his clothes, plastic tubes were snaking out of nearly every body orifice, and he was the colour of tripe. I looked at his chart, and wished I hadn't. 'His blood pressure . . .' I stammered.

'Hasn't worsened,' said the male nurse, another infant, who hadn't even started shaving yet. 'Look, he's young, he's well nourished, he's got a good chance . . .'

'What are his injuries?' Brian asked.

'We won't know until we get the x-rays. Certainly a broken leg and maybe a fractured skull.'

I remember thinking why 'broken' for leg and 'fractured' for skull? Shock plays some strange tricks. Then the Sister brought Marcus's crash helmet. It didn't seem possible that our nerves could take any more hammering, but at the sight of the cracked helmet, Brian's face went a sort of porcelain texture, and I felt my knees buckle. The Sister managed to get chairs under us before we hit the deck.

I wish every young motorcyclist who supports the 'anti-helmet' campaign could be made to look at a helmet *after* an accident. Marcus's helmet, which was rock hard to the touch, now had a deep gash, like a rift valley, running from the neck to the top of the dome. And if he hadn't been wearing it? It would have been what I believe they call a shovel job.

Brian went into an office to sign a consent form, leaving me with Marcus and the male nurse. The nurse smiled encouragingly – a genuine smile; he was too young to have developed a professional one – and said 'He looks tough, he won't give up easily.'

'He's very stubborn,' I said. 'He's a Taurus.'

'One of the best signs,' said the nurse. 'You go home and try to get some rest. We'll phone you directly there's any change.'

'Goodbye Marcus,' I whispered to the dummy on the bed. I squeezed his hand. *'And get back into your body.'*

On the way home we were jerked out of our dreamlike state by the sight of an overturned car in the middle of the main road. Brian rescued the trapped driver, and we sat him in our car until the police came swishing through the driving rain. It's an ill wind all right, we told each other when we arrived home light-headed and giggling hysterically.

In the days that followed we were overwhelmed by the kindness and concern shown not only by our friends and relations, but also by the village community. The garage owner lent us a reliable car free of charge; complete strangers phoned up to ask after Marcus, and Ursula came in every day to puppy-sit and man the phone while we visited the hospital. Sara came home and the three of us lived on tea and toast, lost weight, and snapped each others' heads off. We weren't very good at living with stress.

Marcus had a broken head, a dislocated neck and a broken arm and leg. He regained consciousness but had taken a time-trip and thought it was still 1969. We had some rather Alice in Wonderland conversations with him, mainly about the shortcomings of Alf Ramsey as England's manager. He remembered nothing about the day of the accident and still doesn't, seven years later.

The policeman who saved his life said that Marcus had had a head-on collision with a car, whose driver probably failed to dip his lights. The car was unlicensed, un-MOT'd and uninsured. Marcus had been thrown right over the top of the car and had landed face down in a farm gateway. When the policeman got to him, Marcus's face was embedded in the mud, and his heart had stopped. His saviour had given him the kiss of life and heart massage. In the ambulance his heart stopped again and the ambulance men cranked it back into action.

Three weeks later he came home, complete with surgical collar and two limbs in plaster. He was back in present time mentally, but was uncharacteristically aggressive. This, we learned later, was perfectly normal behaviour after a crack on the head, but it was an awful strain at the time.

There were a few children booked in for half term, all girls and all under eleven. This wasn't going to be much fun for Marcus, immobilised in a chair all day and feeling a fool. Luckily we were able to borrow the twenty-year-old son of some friends for a week. His name was Julian and he too had a broken leg, plastered to the thigh.

Julian was a relaxed friendly lad, popular with the little girls and a real asset to us. He never minded letting the children clamber all over him or write on his plaster. Marcus, though, found the constant giggling intolerable and would hit the children with his crutches and make them cry. I bought a crate of Guinness for the boys to build their strengths up. One day, unnerved by the silence coming from the playroom, I went to investigate.

Julian and Marcus were playing chess and all the little girls were asleep on floor cushions.

'Good heavens,' I said. 'They don't usually have a sleep in the afternoon.'

'We gave them some Guinness,' Marcus grinned. 'Worked a treat.'

I pelted upstairs to Brian who was papering the bathroom. 'Brian! They're *plastered*!'

'Of course they are.' Brian went on papering.

'Not the *boys*, the *children*. They're stewed.'

'Stewed?'

'Stoned, drunk, blotto. They've been at the Guinness.'

Brian climbed down the ladder. 'Little girls don't drink Guinness,' he said.

He changed his tune when he saw the empty bottles. 'Christ,' he said. 'I wouldn't have thought they'd like the taste.'

'Suppose the parents come a day early to fetch them?' I said. 'How could we explain this away?'

Brian surveyed the heap of inebriated infants thoughtfully and prodded one with his toe.

'Don't wake that one up, Brian, please,' Marcus begged.

'Don't be daft, I'm going to wake them all up,' said Brian.

'Well, leave Lois till last then,' said Marcus. 'She's such a pest.' Lois, a ferrety looking seven-year-old, had developed a crush on Marcus, and was always wanting to comb his hair. Marcus called her 'Lois Common Denominator' and 'Lois Form of Life' but Lois, who was a bit dim, overlooked any nastiness on her hero's part, and continued to hover round him with a brush and comb at the ready.

'I'll make them some hot milk and honey,' I said. 'I believe honey's good for hangovers.' Soon all the little girls were sipping their drinks as they watched Blue Peter. Apart from their flushed faces, they seemed none the worse for their binge and Brian was all in favour of making it a daily ritual. 'Imagine when the summer children come,' he said. 'We could give them all a slug after lunch and they wouldn't surface till supper.'

The children were collected by their parents the next day and no reference was made to yesterday's mishap. Each parent was hauled to the playroom to admire its own daughter's art work on the boys' plasters. The playroom had been tidied so that it no longer looked like a saloon bar, just a men's surgical ward.

'So much extra work for you,' the mothers murmured sympathetically. 'You should have told us — we could have postponed the children's holiday.'

'They've been no trouble at all,' we assured them, thinking of the latest red missive from the bank. 'It's been a pleasure.'

Lois's mother said, 'I don't know how you keep them occupied on rainy days, I run out of ideas at home.' Marcus and Julian exchanged a conspiratorial look and kept mum.

Brian, with phone clamped between chin and shoulder, lit a cigarette and made a note on the telephone pad. He said questioningly, 'The *right* way to shoot a goat? And butchery? Oh, I see. Bye.' He replaced the receiver and turned to me. 'They're throwing us in at the deep end. We're going to shoot goats.'

'Have you flipped your lid? Who's going to shoot goats?'

'We are. It's our first course.'

'With strangled bantam for pudding, I suppose?'

'Not that sort of course. A Smallholders' Association course. Educational.'

'Oh, the Smallholders' Association. Why didn't you say so?'

A few weeks previously we had attended the inaugural meeting of a group of smallholders. A committee had been set up, various educational bodies contacted and a name decided upon. Various suggestions like Smallholders in Training had been discarded because the initial letters did not look nice on letter-headed stationery. So the Smallholders' Association had been born and the members, nearly all of whom were educated but ignorant townies like ourselves, were eagerly looking forward to a packed programme of instructive and social meetings.

Quite a few members kept goats and sent the surplus males to slaughterhouses. It was felt that it would be more humane to have them killed at home than subject them to the horrors of the abbatoir. This then was what Brian had meant by 'throwing us in at the deep end'. We were going to be instructed by a licensed slaughterer not only on how to shoot an animal correctly but also how to eviscerate and butcher the carcass.

The course took place on the small farm of one of the members. About twelve of us turned up feeling rather ghoulish, but determined to be tough. A goat was led out, tethered, and shot. Just like that. The goat knew nothing and all we suffered was a ringing in the ears from the deafening bang of the rifle. Talking among ourselves afterwards, we all agreed that we were surprised at our lack of reaction, considering none of us had had any experience of first-hand killing.

'Mind you,' someone said, 'if that had been my Ferdie, I might not have been so cool.'

'The trouble with you lot,' said the instructor, 'is that you will *name* your male animals. You only make it harder for yourselves.'

Thinking of Charles and Adam, our two sheep whose labelled joints reproached me every time I opened the freezer, I nodded agreement.

'I can't eat my pig Bernard,' said one girl. 'I reared him on the bottle from a day old. I'm going to swap him with my friend's Prendergast.'

'Posh name for a pig.'

'He's a posh pig — a Tamworth. Bernard's a Landrace, so we'll have to make some sort of cash adjustment.'

While this and similar conversations were taking place, the dead goat had been carried into a shed and hung from a beam in the roof. Some of us who had been smugly congratulating ourselves on our composure at the shooting had the smiles wiped off our faces when the instructor eviscerated the goat and caught the steaming entrails in strategically placed buckets. The smell was so overpoweringly sweet and heavy that one or two of us had to go outside for a lungful of the sharp December air.

All the men stayed in the shed, the pipe smokers among them enjoying a sudden surge of popularity. Requests to 'blow a bit my way' would have made a novel tobacco commercial only it might have been difficult to compose a jingle to match the occasion. Once the interior and skin of the goat had been dealt with, we fresh-air fiends rejoined the course to learn how to cut up and joint the meat. This was much harder than it looked when the instructor did it, and nearly all of us produced joints that didn't even faintly resemble those in butchers' shops. We optimistically labelled our offerings 'stewing' or 'roast' although 'dustbin' would have been more appropriate.

The job was eventually finished and the group invited indoors for a wash and much needed cup of tea. We all chatted away enthusiastically and agreed that it had been quite an eye opener. Everyone was thirsting for more courses; we wanted demonstrations on everything from chicken-plucking to castration. Someone said he wanted to learn how to use heavy horses on his small acreage. Brian groaned and said we had four horses whose sixteen heavy feet gave him ulcers every time he looked at the paddock. A tall, dark-haired girl overheard him and came over.

'Hullo. I'm Chris. Do you want some grazing for your horses?'

'Grazing?' Brian gasped. 'You've got grass?'

Chris laughed. 'Yes, I know it sounds unlikely after that drought, but our place is terribly boggy in places, and it never got completely parched. We've got to drain it this winter and we'd like it heavily grazed before we start. Preferably for a month or two.'

To a smallholder, the prospect of two months' rest for one's grass is like winning the pools. Eagerly we snapped up the offer before someone else got to hear of it. We exchanged phone numbers with Chris and drove home through freezing fog singing 'Oh, what a beautiful morning'.

Next day, we visited Chris and met her husband Rob, who was a teacher. They had bought their fifteen-acre holding a short time previously and were too broke to stock it yet — a familiar story among SHA members as it turned out.

'When would you like to bring them over?' Rob asked, when we had beaten the bounds and were thawing out in their miniscule kitchen.

'Would next Monday suit? We've got friends coming for the weekend, and they'll want to go riding if the weather's good enough.'

Our friends, Sue and Keith, arrived at seven o'clock on Friday evening. They had left work early and driven from London to Devon in torrential rain. It had become a standing joke that their visits always coincided with some domestic upheaval at our place — either someone was giving birth or a gate had collapsed or, as latterly, Marcus was battling on a life-support machine. Anyway, this visit proved to be no exception. We had a flood.

They stepped out of their heated car straight into six inches of water. 'You've got a flood,' Keith remarked observantly as his shoes filled with water.

'I don't believe it, I just don't believe it,' said Sue, grabbing a brush and bucket. 'Do you save things up till we come?'

'It's the drain,' Brian explained. 'It's forgotten how, after the drought.'

'Have you got rods?'

'Yes, over there. But we must get the water out of the hall before it reaches the carpets.' The four of us swept and ladled the water out of the hall, then Brian ran to the stables for paper sacks to lay inside the front door. Keith rodded the drain until it gave a great belch, whereupon all the water in the front yard whooshed down the hole and disappeared.

'Marvellous. Thanks for the muscle, people,' said Brian.

'All part of the service,' Keith said, ducking out into the rain to fetch their cases. He returned to find Sue being welcomed by Parsley's puppies. Sue had taken off her wet shoes and all five pups were attacking her bare feet.

'Aren't they gorgeous, Keith? I forgot they'd have their eyes open by now.'

'And their bowels,' said Keith, stepping carefully across the floor.

'I'm training them,' I said hopefully.

'Very successfully it seems,' Brian agreed. 'They're the champion turd producers of all time.' The champions romped across the newspaper and clamoured to be picked up.

'They've been dying to see what you've been doing in the hall,' Marcus said, pouring tea with his good arm. 'They were all lined up with their noses under the door, it was hilarious.'

'How are you, Marcus?' asked Sue.

'Not too bad, thanks. My neck hurts like hell and I keep getting headaches, but my arm and leg are mending. I've got so much comfrey inside me I feel like a compost heap.'

'I knew it would come in useful,' I said. 'I don't often get a chance to use my herbal remedies.'

'Anything to oblige,' said Marcus. 'I'll catch pneumonia if you like so that you can use that ghastly old goose grease you've been hoarding.'

'We're sending him to an osteopath in London next week,' said Brian. 'That surgical collar's useless and Neil — that's our osteopath friend — wants to realign Marcus's neck before it gets too fixed.'

'That's good, that should stop the headaches. How are the boys?'

The 'boys' were Sue and Keith's ponies, Monty and Wellington, who lived with us for mutual convenience. Sue and Keith rode them in term time and we had the use of them for the holiday children.

'They're fine. Wellie's been up to his usual tricks. He turned on the yard tap and left it running for hours, *and* he trapped his foot in something and had to have a new shoe.'

'Is he all right?' said Sue. 'We'd like to go hunting tomorrow.' Brian stared at them. 'Have you heard the weather forecast for tomorrow? Heavy rain and something force winds.'

'We don't mind if the ponies don't,' said Keith, 'and we've had a rehearsal just now with your flood.'

We drank tea and talked until quite late. Sue and Keith brought news of the wider world and we told them about forming the Smallholders' Association and all the new people we had met. Small's kitten, Smallest, was winkled out of the airing cupboard and admired; Sue had found a good home for her with an office colleague and would be taking the kitten back with them.

'I shall miss her,' I said as we watched Smallest wrestle with a boa constrictor under the chair.

'You should sell her to Spurs,' Marcus said. 'She's magic with a ping pong ball.'

Next day Sue and Keith went hunting in the promised torrential rain, returning at three o'clock soaked and ravenous. 'Something smells good,' said Keith, lifting the lid of my biggest saucepan. 'What's this?'

'Bran mash with cod-liver oil and pony nuts.'

'Makes a change from boring old roast beef and Yorkshire pudding, I suppose,' said Keith.

'Did you catch any foxes?'

'No. Didn't even see any. The ponies were super — they went like the clappers.'

'I thought they might. I gave them oats last night.'

'*You* gave them oats?' Brian said in alarm. 'I gave them oats too.'

'How come? You don't feed the ponies.'

'No, but I wanted some paper sacks for the hall floor. There were some oats left in a feed bag, so I tipped the lot into Monty and Wellie's manger.'

'Good grief, no wonder they went like the clappers,' I said. 'They could have gone to Mars and back on double oats.'

Sue, towelling her hair, said 'What are you all laughing at?'

'The ponies had four star fuel yesterday. It seems we're lucky to be here,' said Keith.

'Since we are here, I suggest we all sit down and eat,' Brian said. 'I'll carve the bran mash.'

Chapter Five

SITTING UP IN BED sharing tea and biscuits with five fat friends is quite the nicest way to start the day. The puppies looked forward to the ritual as much as I did, and would gallop along the landing in front of Brian who was carrying the tea tray, and stand on their hind legs clawing at the bedclothes until I helped them on to the bed. Then they would make sure I stayed awake by biting my nose and ears, or seeing if they could tug my hair out by the roots. Two digestive biscuits had to be distributed – one for me and one between five of them. One into five doesn't go – well, not very tidily – and by the time they were ten weeks old, Brian was making noises about taking what was left of the pillow and moving into a spare room until they were sold.

'And it's not just the damage they're doing,' he said one particularly stressful day, when Clover had pulled the phone on to the floor and Kickstart had gone punk with some yellow paint. 'They must be costing a fortune to feed now.' I knew to a penny what they were costing to feed and lived in hope of finding a butcher to have an affair with so that I could get cheap ox heart.

'I don't want to sell them before Christmas.' Or after Christmas or ever. 'They might end up as presents.' Ending up as presents was a danger we hadn't thought of when we had had Parsley mated in August.

'Don't be stupid,' Brian said, dabbing Araldite on to the broken phone pieces. 'Put an ad in the paper and vet the buyers.'

Vet them I did. Dealers of course were OUT, rather rudely in some cases, but Brian had made a good job of glueing the phone together, and the joins held. Parents with toddlers were out too; my carefully reared puppies were not going to be pulled about like toys. One man phoned saying he wanted a pup for 'the wife' as they had had a quarrel and he wanted to make it up before Christmas, so I suggested a cashmere sweater and added his name to the 'not suitable' list. Brian got pretty stroppy about that one and reminded me that he himself had bought Parsley as a present for me.

'That was different,' I said. 'You don't call me "the wife".'

'You'll be the ex-wife if you lumber us with seven dogs. Christ, I didn't think people would have to pass a test in semantics before they bought a dog.' He was somewhat mollified when a discerning couple, holidaying in Devon, came to choose a puppy and, finding the charms of Kickstart and Revvup equally irresistible, bought both.

'Their credentials OK, were they?' Brian said, not too sarcastically when he saw how much I missed the two tearaways.

'Yes, it'll be a super home,' I said. 'They've got a couple of dogs already and plenty of space. They're going to call the pups Byron and Boswell.'

Nutmeg went next to comfort a couple whose fifteen-year-old labrador had died. They were no longer youngsters themselves and wanted a smaller dog. Nutmeg, normally the shyest of the litter, trotted across to them as soon as they came into the house and rolled over to show what four square meals a day could do to a chap's figure. They couldn't wait to get him home to fill the vacuum left by the labrador.

Brian sold Clover one day when I was out and lived to tell the tale. Yes, they were nice people, he kept assuring me, no they didn't have toddlers, yes they did have a big garden and will you shut up for five minutes and *listen*. 'They're coming back tomorrow to meet you, I told them you'd skin me alive not knowing where Clover's gone.'

'Why couldn't they take her tomorrow? What's the hurry?'

'They couldn't resist her. You know the way she puts her head on one side and her ears . . .'

'Please,' I sniffed. Brian gave me his hanky. 'They're coming in the morning,' he said.

I spent a miserable night picturing Clover shut in some draughty shed whining for her mother. Clover, on the other hand, slept well under the eiderdown of her new owners, who turned out to be as nice as Brian said they were.

Caraway became our shadow after his brothers and sister had gone. Just before the relationship reached the point of no return, he was bought by a family who farmed near Bridgwater. Tony shod the family horses once a month and not only vouched for them as puppy owners but was also able to give us monthly bulletins on Caraway's progress.

It was awful without the puppies, but what with the pigs farrowing – Rosie on Christmas Day and Phyll on Boxing Day – and Sara coming home for Christmas; and several Smallholders' Association meetings to attend, life was too hectic to brood for long. It snowed during Sara's stay and we made a Cresta Run down the steep drive, with straw bales at the bottom to stop the sledges. Our osteopath friend had mended Marcus's neck and the headaches had stopped, but he was still terribly irritable and insisted on having a few goes on a sledge to cheer himself up. I would not recommend sledging as a therapy for fracture cases, although in fact he managed very well considering he had an arm and a leg in plaster. He cheered up no end, which was more than we did after pulling him and his sledge all the way to the top a few times.

'Come back ponies, all is forgiven,' Brian gasped, as the three of us prepared to haul the sledges up again. But the ponies were still enjoying their holiday with our new friends, Chris and Rob, and were not available for husky services.

The snow thawed before we all got hernias and Sara went back to London, having arranged for Marcus to join her when he was out of plaster. He was undecided about resuming work in Exeter because of the long journey each day and talked of getting a transfer to London. Meanwhile he manned the phone for us, a service which suddenly became a full time job . . .

Way back in August, a television unit from the BBC had made a short film at our place as part of a series they were making about children's holidays. The film was to be shown on the Nationwide programme, but when, nobody seemed to know. 'Some time in December,' said a spokesman at the BBC in answer to our query, so there was nothing for it but to wheel the television into the kitchen and watch Nationwide every day. How we hated it, not Nationwide itself – that was just

39

boring with its seemingly endless succession of trade union people arguing the toss with stuffed shirts — but the fact of having to give up a precious half hour each day to watch anything.

TV in the kitchen is a Bad Thing. Death to conversation and digestion and a danger to flex-chewing puppies. By mid-December, I could have heaved a brick through the screen, then Brian had the bright idea of turning the sound off so that we could listen to Radio 4 and keep an eye open for 'our' film. We endured this schizophrenic half hour every day for a month, until at last in January our stoicism was rewarded.

'We're on! Quick, you two,' Brian leapt for the volume control, I took the phone off the hook and Marcus switched off the radio. 'And later in the programme,' said the announcer, 'we'll be showing you another film in our series on holidays for unaccompanied children.'

In an agony of suspense we sat through yet another trade union altercation — why they're called unions when they're anything but united I can't imagine. 'GET OFF, you boring old fart,' Brian shook his fist at one of Her Majesty's ministers, and to our surprise he did, and the title music came on to herald the holiday film series with our calf in close up being bottle-fed by one of our holiday guests.

'There's Garry. Why was the calf on the bottle?'

'He wasn't, we did it for the film crew. Ssh.'

'There's *me*,' said Marcus. 'Wasn't I brown?'

'Ssh.'

The film made Phyllishayes look very appealing. The parched brown fields with their huge drought-caused fissures didn't look as bad as we had feared because one's attention was focused on all the activities. Brightly clad children rode shiny coated ponies, fed baby animals, cuddled rabbits and fought in the hay. There was a particularly beautiful scene at the river with the children splashing and laughing, then an unbeautiful scene of me in Brian's best blue shirt being interviewed.

'That's my check shirt,' said Brian indignantly. 'Who said you could have my shirt?'

'Ssh, please, we'll miss something.' Actually I think I could have done without the sight of myself, with brillo pad hair, making fatuous remarks to the interviewer. Then back to the children; more feeding, themselves this time.

'Do you remember the sausages and ice cream?'

'Ssh. This next bit's Jeremy.' And there was sweet Jeremy, everyone's favourite eight-year-old with enough Irish charm to melt granite and a gap-toothed grin which had great purchasing power.

'Didn't we spoil that monster?' said Brian.

'Yes, didn't we just,' I agreed nostalgically.

Jeremy, wearing a Nationwide printed T-shirt (he was the son of one of the Nationwide presenters) gave a polished performance for the camera. He collected eggs from the nest boxes, fed the baby goats, rode a pony and answered questions from the interviewer unselfconsciously. The film finished with another close up of the bottle-fed calf, then the announcer held up a booklet and said full details of this and other holidays for unaccompanied children were included in this booklet. This was a joint publication by the British Tourist Board and the BBC and was available in most bookshops.

Scarcely twenty minutes after the broadcast the phone rang. It was a parent wanting to book in two children for two weeks in August. She hadn't waited for the full details promised in the pamphlet. Nor had the next caller or the next or the next. By bedtime we had nine provisional bookings and might have had more if our own friends and relatives had not swamped the phone wanting to talk about the film.

'Good old Nationwide,' said Marcus, as we put out the lights and headed for bed. Brian agreed, but couldn't help feeling — albeit guiltily — that it would be nice not to have to watch it tomorrow.

'Maybe when we're rich and leisured we'll watch it from choice,' I said, trying to placate the gods.

'Do they get Nationwide in the Bahamas?' said Brian.

Next day we got the GPO to put a long flex on the telephone so that Marcus could take calls from the sitting room instead of the uncomfortable lobby in the kitchen. One of the first messages he took was from a primary school in London who wanted to book twenty children and three staff for a week in June. 'It's a Catholic school,' he said, handing us the phone pad, 'and they're sending a nun.'

'A *nun*?' We stared at him in consternation.

'And that's not all,' said Marcus, enjoying the impact his message had had. 'The nun wants to *ride a horse*.'

Well, words failed me. A nun — a being as alien as a dinosaur — was sensational enough, but a *riding* nun? Words didn't fail Brian or Marcus though. 'We'll have to get a horse called Grace, so she'll have something to fall from,' started the ball rolling, and the two masters of corn soon had us knee deep in jokes about habits, monks and confessions.

We didn't really believe in the riding nun, until the completed booking form came back from the school. But there, on the list of names of those wishing to ride was Sister Bridget, plain as plain. How, we wondered, were we going to get her mounted? Her robes would not only get in the way, they would frighten the horses. I phoned a friend of mine, Belinda, who used to be a Catholic before she went to art school, and asked her if I should try to borrow a side saddle for Sister Bridget.

'You really are an idiot,' Belinda said, when she had finished having a good laugh at my expense. 'The Sister will wear slacks, same as anybody else when she's riding.'

'A nun in slacks? Are you sure they're allowed?'

'Yes, quite. She's in a teaching Order, so she probably wears mufti a lot of the time. Just remember to give them fish on Fridays and give the Sister a private room for her devotions and everything will be fine. Anyway, I don't know why you're worrying about it in January, they're not coming until June.'

Now it was my turn for a jeer. Belinda might be well versed in religious matters, but had a lot to learn about running a guest house. It was *only* by forward planning that a guest house could function at all. This we had learned the hard way during our first season and knew now that even a minor item like a hired side saddle, if fixed up in January, could be one less unit of stress avoided later on. Things that seemingly run on oiled wheels, like a perfect dinner party or a P.G. Wodehouse book, are a tribute to the hours put in beforehand arranging the peanuts or discarding subordinate clauses. Not that I can claim to be a dab hand with peanuts or clauses, but it's something you have to aim for.

Brian was busy with his own forward planning – the garden. The best bit of the gardener's year had started for him and soon the sitting-room floor was strewn with seed catalogues and lists. Last year's drought had ruined most growing crops and he was determined to get two years' fun from the catalogues to compensate. Admiral Beatty, Cook's Delight, Tender and True, Cherry Belle and Powder Puff begged to be among the chosen few as did Early Nantes, Giant Zittan, The Prince, Desirée and Rosie Frills.

Marcus and I caught the list bug and started ones on motor-bikes and dogs respectively. Marcus's bike had been a write-off after the accident and he wanted a replacement. If he had been a tearaway type Brian and I would have banned another bike, but as he was a cautious self-preserving sort of boy, we smiled encouragingly and coped with our ulcers in private.

My dog list had to be a more furtive project than the men-folks'. Honey was nearly eleven years old, quite crabby in damp weather and no fun for visiting children. She won't be with us much longer, I reasoned, (I'm still saying the same thing and Honey is in her seventeenth year), and we need another dog to play with the children. I hid my lists down the sofa cushions but old Hawkeye found them, together with five dog books from the library.

'*Another* dog,' he ranted, as if we had twenty. 'What the hell do we want another dog for? I haven't recovered from Parsley's puppies yet.' Parsley, hearing her name, thumped her tail on the floor. She knows what sound and fury signify.

'Honey's old and irritable,' I explained. 'She doesn't play with the children any more.'

'I'm old and irritable,' Brian interrupted, 'and *I* have to play with them. Give her an aspirin or something. Everyone's got to pull their weight around here.' Five minutes later he was absentmindedly fondling Honey's ears and crooning some ghastly sentimental old lyric about 'Nobody loves you when you're old and grey' while he filled in his Suttons order form.

Choosing the breed of our new dog took ages. Just as I thought I had cracked it, Brian or Marcus or Sara (consulted by phone) would give my choice the thumbs down. We all agreed that terriers were out, as were toy dogs, working dogs, and hounds. With this narrowed field we ended up with a short list of three – Golden Retriever, Standard Poodle or Rough Collie. Retrievers had plate-sized, mud-holding feet according to Brian and Marcus said poodles needed a haircut every month.

'We're having a collie,' I told Sara on a cheap-rate evening phone call.

'Great. Merle, tricolour or sable?'

'Sable,' I said, gazing at a picture of a sable collie in a dog book.

'Don't forget to check on both parents' temperaments. *And* hip displasia.' Sara knew almost as much about dogs as she thought she did.

It's a funny thing about buying and selling, the thing you want is always in short supply, whereas if you're on the selling end there's usually a glut of your product. So it was with our collie; we had to go on the waiting list of the breeder we chose. Our puppy (not even born when we reserved her) would be ready at the end of April, leaving three months to settle and train her before the bulk of the children arrived in August.

Meanwhile, the Smallholders' Association was taking up more and more of our time, and we started getting up in what seemed like the middle of the night in order to get our jobs done and leave time to attend day courses. The Association had taken off with a bang and had attracted the media. 'West Country Smallholders form a Co-operative' proclaimed one paper inaccurately, and 'Bartering is Fun' said another, rather more accurately. Then two TV companies sent camera crews to find out what made our members tick and they went away with some hilarious footage of film. There was one scene where two members who were going to swap venison for trout were filmed walking towards each other with their offerings. They met, swapped and retreated without saying a word, as they were struck dumb by the presence of the camera. It was like *High Noon* without the guns.

Someone once described the SHA members as the 'nouveau poor' and this was pretty accurate. Very few of us had new clothes, holidays or posh cars, but when it came to food we all lived like kings. Leaving aside the nutters and dilettantes, whom most clubs attract, we as a group found we had a common pool of eggs, chickens, lamb, milk, cream, butter, cheese, beef, pork, rabbit, venison, pheasant, trout, and fresh vegetables. By bartering, anyone could fill his freezer with the foods of his choice and, if he didn't happen to have the item that his barter partner wanted, he could enter into a three- or even four-way transaction. For instance: A wants a duck from B. B wants some fencing posts which only C can supply, but C doesn't want a duck. A therefore lends her teenage son to muck out C's cowhouse. C gives B the fencing posts as payment and B gives a duck to A. It looks complicated but is very simple really.

Brian and I swapped three Maran hens, a sack of parsnips and a week's decorating for a secondhand van and two bantams. A TV reporter was on hand to record the handing over of the bartered items and, when one of the bantams laid an egg during filming, raised the nice legal point — who owns the egg? (An arbiter decided the bantam owned the egg.)

Over the next couple of years Bristol University and the Agricultural Training Board took an interest in the SHA and laid on professional tuition for us in many aspects of animal husbandry and horticulture. But for the present, we arranged farm walks on each others' holdings, social and educational evenings, and invaluable one-day events where we learned the rudiments of the subject in hand. Many blissful hours were spent releasing smelly pus from the feet of infected sheep (The Sheep Course) and learning what went on in the multiple stomachs of a cow (Slide-Illustrated Vet Talk).

It was a pity that 'Table Preparation of Poultry' was scheduled for the autumn, as we had twenty chickens ready for killing and only an academic grasp of how to do it. 'Easy,' said Tony, when we put our problem to him. 'I'll show you. Not squeamish, are you?'

'No,' said Brian bravely, and watched with mounting nausea as Tony killed ten chickens in as many seconds. Brian did the next ten and was so fearful in case he only half-killed them he overdislocated some of them and was left with a body in one hand and a head in the other.

'It's a good fault,' said Tony kindly. 'At least you're sure they're dead.' He slung the chickens neatly over a beam in the

45

barn and instructed us to start plucking. 'Don't leave them too long,' he said. 'Cold plucking's a terrible job.' Then he drove away, leaving us surveying the row of birds apprehensively.

It took us the whole of that day and part of the evening to pluck the twenty, and would have taken even longer if Shirley (the friend with no stairs), dropping in to say hullo, hadn't come to our rescue. She sent her daughter Patricia to help us. 'She's done a poultry course at the Young Farmers' Club,' said Shirley. 'She's very competent.'

Competence was obviously hereditary in Shirley's family, and under Patricia's guidance we learned how to pluck the feathers without flaying the birds. Our fingers were sore for days afterwards. Patricia then showed us how to eviscerate and at this point Brian copped out, which was fair enough as he'd done the killing. 'I'll make some more tea,' he said as the buckets began to fill with entrails. Strangely enough, I found I didn't mind delving around inside abdominal cavities, and was fascinated when Patricia pointed out the oviducts with their clusters of tiny eggs queueing up on a sort of production line. Eventually the job was done; Patricia went home with a chicken as a thank-you present, and we loaded the remaining nineteen into the freezer. They were magnificent birds, some weighing over 10 lb, and well worth the care we had lavished on them for the past few months.

Next day it was our turn to answer an SOS. A farmer friend called Reg had gone down with pneumonia and his wife, Polly, with six children under twelve and a milking herd to see to was not her usual slapdash self. 'I can manage the milking,' she said, 'but I can't cut the silage or see to the slurry. Tony's offered to come in every day for an hour or so, but I wonder if Brian could do the morning silage for me until Reg is better.'

Brian and Tony kept the outside operations running as smoothly as possible, and I gave Polly a hand in the house and did some of her shopping for her. Reg's recovery seemed slow; his bedroom was situated above the kitchen, and we could hear his painful coughing spasms from there.

'What does the doctor say?' I asked Polly, about ten days after the onset of the illness.

'He says Reg has got to rest.'

'What about medicine?'

'*Useless*, that medicine,' said Polly scornfully. 'I tried it on that calf — you know, the one with pneumonia — and it was dead in the morning. Useless. So I threw it away.'

'You gave the *calf* Reg's medicine?'

'Yes. Pneumonia's pneumonia, isn't it? Good job it was the calf that died, could have been poor Reg, couldn't it?'

Poor Reg indeed. He was lucky Polly hadn't called the vet to the calf first or goodness knows what the outcome might have been. In the event, deprived of his antibiotics, he dosed himself with the sort of medicine that makes you mellow and within a month he was as good as new.

With all these extra-mural activities going on, we had almost forgotten about the guest-house side of things, then one day, just as we were planning to attend an evening lecture (Cereals and Grasses) a German woman rang up. We *must* help her. The British Tourist Board had recommended us. She had a family crisis on her hands. Carl and Rolf were on their way.

Chapter Six

GLUMLY WE lingered over lunch, looking forward to the Germans' visit with as much enthusiasm as Churchill in 1939. Carl and Rolf arrived with their mother by taxi at about four o'clock, by which time we had pulled ourselves together enough to be courteous if not gushing.

The mother was a highly strung woman, thin as a stick, and in the ten minutes or so she was with us – she had kept her taxi waiting outside – she tried to explain why she was leaving her sons at such short notice. We couldn't make out a quarter of the tale, which involved a diplomat husband (confusingly called Carl also), who was being posted somewhere to stop or start an uprising. And she, the mother, had to be in Luxembourg or Heidelberg, for the funeral of some VIP, who had inconvenienced everyone by dying when he was supposed to be getting better.

Then she would be joining her husband at the scene of the revolution, and would phone the boys every day. She was away in the taxi, in a flurry of *Auf Wiedersehens* before we had time to get her European address or to discuss payment.

'*Auf Wiedersehen, Mutti; grüsse Vati herzlich von uns.*'

'*Auf Wiedersehen, meine Schätze. Morgen werde ich anrufen.*'

We waved the taxi goodbye, and went indoors to take stock of each other. Carl was a strikingly handsome twelve-year-old and Rolf, also good-looking, was ten. They were tall, fair and brown-eyed, with the sort of dazzling white teeth you usually associate with Americans. So far so good. We had supper and during the meal discovered that the boys were as baffled as we were about their mother's tour of Europe. Both boys spoke excellent English, much to our relief, as our German comprised two sentences: 'I will ring for a maid' and 'My horse has the colic' neither of which was very useful.

'Our mother is excitable,' said Carl. 'She is always doing something in a hurry. How long are we to stay here?'

'Don't worry, Carl,' I said. 'I don't suppose it'll be for long.'

'No. You misunderstand,' said Carl. 'I would like to stay here a long time. I am lazy and I wish to be absent for the end of term tests. I have done no preparation at all. Neither has Rolf.'

'Our school is very strict,' said Rolf. 'We do not like it.' The family had been living in London for some years, and the children went to a day school for overseas pupils.

'How much do you pay for sausages?' asked Rolf suddenly. Brian and I thought perhaps he was trying out a sentence from a text-book, and glared at Marcus who was choking with laughter.

'About 40p a pound, I think,' I replied.

'Wholesale or retail?' persisted Rolf. This surely was no text-book talk.

'Why do you want to know?'

Carl explained, 'He is interested in money. He is going to be a stockbroker when he grows up.'

'How much will you give me for this sausage, Carl?' said Rolf. 'I cannot eat four. Will you give me 6p for this sausage?'

'*Rolf*,' said Brian sharply. 'You can't *sell* your food. What an extraordinary notion. I'll give you some money if you need some.'

'I do not want money this evening. I will have some when we go to the shops,' said Rolf solemnly. We finished supper, gave the spare sausage to Honey and sent the boys to the playroom to watch television. Carl was back in the kitchen immediately.

'Have you another television set, please?' he said. 'The one in the playroom has only a twenty-four inch screen and there is no remote control.'

'Oh dear, only a twenty-four inch screen,' said Marcus sarcastically. 'And no remote control. Dear, dear, it's a hard life for us peasants.'

Carl stared at him levelly: 'With injuries such as yours, you should have the remote control,' he said. 'You should sit still until you are better.'

'Listen mate –' Marcus began, but Brian cut in.

'OK. That's enough. Go and watch television, Carl, or read a book until bedtime. I'm coming in to watch the news at nine.'

'I prefer News at Ten,' said Carl. 'I like to see the commercials.'

It was with difficulty that we got the boys to bed at nine o'clock. Most kids away from home try it on – I always stay up until midnight, etc – but in the case of Carl and Rolf we had a sneaking suspicion it might have been true.

Next day, their mother phoned from Strasbourg. She would be attending the funeral the day after tomorrow, and how were her darling sons. 'Such a comfort to me with Carl always travelling. . .' She started to get into her stride but, mindful of the unreliability of long distance calls, I brought her back to practical matters. Like how long were the boys staying? She didn't know, Carl's business was so complicated. Fair enough. How much pocket money did they normally get? Anything they ask for, the darlings. Didn't we think they were the sweetest boys?

'Yes, very sweet, but please give me an idea about their spending money. A pound, five pounds a week?'

'I really don't know,' she apologised. 'I take them to shops where I have accounts and they buy their own things. My husband sees to the bills.'

How wonderful, I thought, and had visions of taking a blank cheque to Harrods. A blue Persian kitten, Chanel No. 5, a pair of real leather riding boots. . . 'Oh, and another thing, Mrs S – the boys need wellingtons. Shall I buy them and put it on the bill?'

'Yes, yes, anything. What is a wellington?' She pronounced it vellington, which made me giggle as did the idea of a single wellington.

'Rubber boots,' I said. 'It's rather muddy here. Rains a lot.'

'They will not go out in the rain, they will take cold. But buy the vellington by all means. I will speak to Carl and Rolf now, please.'

Carl and Rolf spoke to their mother at some length in German. Very frustrating. But they were cheerful enough when they rang off and demanded to be taken shopping. They strutted round Freeman, Hardy and Willis in their green wellingtons chanting 'We are peasants' which was not very sensible coming from a diplomat's children, but in other shops their manners were adequate. They each wanted a stamp album – only the best – but I was blowed if I was going to fork out over twenty pounds on a hobby which would probably be a nine days' wonder, and made them have cheap ones. Even so, once they had added a beginner's collection of stamps, the bill was nearly nine pounds.

Next day, Rolf complained to his mother that he was being fobbed off with inferior goods, and she asked to speak to me again. 'I think Rolf should have the album of his choice,' she said. 'He is truly interested in stamps and hopes they will appreciate in value. I agree with you about Carl's album though, he is only collecting to compete with Rolf.'

By now, I was fed up with stamps. I went back to Taunton and bought Rolf a leather-bound album and a fiver's worth of stamps. Rolf accepted graciously; he didn't crow about getting his own way which, perversely, annoyed me more than if he had.

But Nemesis was on the way, in the shape of our nephews and nieces who came for half term. Brian was amazed at the way I was looking forward to half term, until he realised that it was the thought of the *ponies* return which was making me so cheerful. I had missed them so much while they had been at Chris and Rob's. As soon as I heard Tony's horse box, I rushed out to help unload them. Rocky, the Shetland, clattered down the ramp first, looking as though he was wearing leg-warmers with his absurd little hooves hidden in the shaggy fur. Then Wellie, the Welsh grey, treading on everyone's feet in his usual careless fashion, followed by Monty, a calm black cob who always looked immaculate whatever the weather. Then Noah.

'Noah!' I flung my arms round my favourite pony, but he wasn't in the mood for a cuddle. He had been in the horse box for a quarter of an hour. *Fifteen whole minutes* without food, he indicated; not good enough, and he tugged at his halter rope and headed towards his stable.

Our family children, Guy, Sassy, Tim, Sally and Emma, tumbled out of the train laden with luggage, riding hats, boots and fishing rods. Sally had a brand new riding crop, a present from her father.

'Daddy caused quite a stir buying it,' she giggled. 'He went into Selfridges before Christmas, you know, when it's all crowded, and he said to an assistant, "I want a whip for a young girl." I mean, can you imagine?' We all roared with laughter but Carl and Rolf remained po-faced, and Carl said: 'Why did he want a whip? Does he beat you?'

'No, stupid. Anyway, it's a crop, not a whip. How are the ponies, Faith? And Marcus, of course,' she added hurriedly.

'Fine. Marcus is having his plasters off this week.'

'Are there any other children coming?'

'Three. Doreen, June and Roger. They're from Yorkshire; their parents run a hotel.'

'Bit of a busman's holiday for them, isn't it?' said Sassy. Brian laughed. 'Phyllishayes is hardly in the same league as a hotel, Sassy.'

'It's *much* nicer than any hotel,' said Sassy loyally. 'It's different. You don't get fetched in vans full of straw bales when you go to hotels.'

'Why have you taken the seats out of the transit, Brian?' asked Guy, opening the van doors and peering in. Guy was Sassy's fourteen-year-old brother, ten foot tall and still growing.

'We're fetching one of the pigs back from the boar soon, she might injure herself on the seats. The straw bales are for you to sit on.'

'Magic,' said Tim, settling himself on the straw.

'M'm, magic,' they all agreed. Brian and I exchanged glances. 'Magic' was obviously this term's word.

'Makes a change from "great",' Brian murmured, and let in the clutch.

Later in the day the Yorkshire children joined us, a rather Hogarthian-looking trio, with outgoing friendly personalities that more than compensated for any physical drawbacks. They used a lot of 'ee oops' before starting a sentence, and this was so infectious we all did it before the end of the holiday. June, the eldest, gave me some useful tips about catering, and showed me how to clean out the deep fryer without turning the kitchen into an oil well.

It was good to have nine children filling the house with energy; good too, that Carl and Rolf were diluted. They were not keen on joining the others when they went riding or fishing or walking, and spent more and more time in the playroom as the weather worsened. Even tack-cleaning on the kitchen table — a favourite wet-day chore with everyone — didn't appeal to them.

'You're awful dismal,' one of the Yorkshire kids told Rolf. 'You cheat at cards, boast about your rich dad and don't clean the bath.' Rolf, the true son of his diplomat father, agreed with the analysis calmly.

'I am not used to your ways,' he said.

But he got his come uppance. One day he took some Monopoly money and put it in his pocket so that he would have a head start when the next game began. His crime was discovered, and the scandalised group debated quickly on the best way of punishing him.

'You're pitiful, Rolf.'

'A right pillock.'

'A germ. A rotten old germ. Let's send him to Coventry.'

'Let's put ice cubes down his jumper.'

'De-bag him.'

'No, that's mucky,' said Doreen primly. 'What do you think, Carl? What would he hate most?'

Rolf looked at his brother imploringly. 'I will give you my stamps, Carl,' he offered. Carl appeared to consider this, but then decided blood wasn't thicker than water.

'What Rolf would hate most,' he said, 'is to go for a walk in the rain. . .'

Brian and I watched Rolf's forlorn figure setting out in his new wellingtons for a two-mile circuit in heavy rain. Roger followed him at a discreet distance to see that he didn't take any short cuts.

After this, Marcus showed him how to play Go For Broke, a

53

much better game than Monopoly. Each player starts off with a million pounds and the winner is the one who can spend all the money first. Carl and Rolf preferred having the money to winning the game so everyone was satisfied.

Marcus's broken arm and leg had knitted well (thanks to my comfrey I always maintain) and the plasters were removed. He was horrified when he saw how wasted his skin had become and started a course of toning exercises with olive oil rubs to get the wrinkles out. He still relied on sticks for going upstairs but felt sufficiently secure to arrange a visit to Sara in London to complete his convalescence. So at the end of the half-term holiday he went back on the train with his London-bound cousins, taking his records, posters, motorbike magazines and a packet of dried comfrey.

Carl and Rolf stayed with us for a further two weeks, becoming more morose as the days passed. They watched far too much television and showed no interest in anything connected with the farm. Each day their mother phoned, promising bigger and better presents for her ewe lambs if they would be good and not keep asking when she was coming home.

As far as we were concerned, we felt we were merely guardians, not holiday hosts and went about our normal routine sometimes including the boys if they could be prised out of the playroom, but otherwise leaving them to their own devices. We had to attend the Smallholders' Association AGM one evening, and with no Marcus to hold the fort, took Carl and Rolf along.

The meeting was held in a member's house, a very nice house with a big drawing room for the fifty or so assembled people and a sitting room with a television set where the boys were supposed to stay quietly. At first everything was fine and we mingled happily with our new friends, talking shop and seeing what was up for sale or barter on the noticeboard.

'I see Betty's selling a stud buck,' said someone at my elbow. 'You and Brian want a buck, don't you?'

'Yes, we do,' I said. 'We're going over to New Zealand Whites instead of crossbreds.' I found Betty instructing a grubby young couple about the timing of goat breeding. What Betty didn't know about goats and rabbits after many years as a breeder of both, wasn't worth knowing.

'You take a piece of cotton rag,' she was saying, 'and rub it over the billy until it's really smelly, then. . .'

'Where, precisely?' demanded the girl. The boy flushed with embarrassment and Betty said airily, 'Oh, genitals, chest, anywhere really where there's a good strong pong. Then you put the rag in a glass jar with an airtight lid, and when you think the nanny's in season you give her a sniff of the rag. If she's ready she'll get excited and if not try again a few hours later.'

'Thank you,' said the girl. She wore a cheesecloth floor-length garment and had dirty toenails. 'We'll try that, won't we darling?' Darling nodded dubiously and the couple wandered off.

'Can I have a word about your buck, Betty?' I said.

'Hamish? He's a two-year-old and his previous owner. . .' Just then the chairman called us to order, and invited us to take our places so that the committee business could begin. 'Speak to you later,' Betty mouthed, and I nodded. The minutes were read and then to our acute embarrassment we heard Carl and Rolf singing 'A-Mars-a-day-makes-your-teeth-all-decay' and other less printable adaptations of TV commercials. Brian was nearest the door and tiptoed out to gag the boys. He returned to his place and all was quiet for ten minutes, then Carl and Rolf started running up and down the stairs to the lavatory, then we heard a cup breaking. Again Brian left the room. The evening was ruined for both of us and, making our apologies to our hosts, we left the meeting before the end, took the boys home and sent them to bed in disgrace.

Next day, we took them with us to collect a hen house we had bought in a sale. They had no intention of helping and lounged around looking like a pair of beautiful Afghan hounds. We were still angry with them for yesterday's behaviour, and ordered them to help lift things. That night they must have told their mother they were being used like slaves because she said in no uncertain terms that growing boys must not lift heavy weights in case they rupture themselves. Within twelve hours she phoned again – this time from London. Would we be so kind as to put her darling boys on the next train to Paddington, please?

The holiday bookings were flooding in by every post, thanks to the TV publicity and a very good write up in two British Tourist Board publications. Our encounter with Carl and Rolf had left us prickly and we had to make a tremendous effort to be equally nice to all the parents who came to vet us. It wasn't easy in the case of the next family, who, by an unfortunate coincidence, were more Germans.

Instead of getting out of their car they just sat there blowing the horn. They had not made an appointment, and we were busy painting the playroom, so we ignored them as we don't believe in answering car horns. Eventually the parents got out and rang the front-door bell. When we answered it there was a small misunderstanding because they thought we were work-men, and then a big misunderstanding when we started to show them round the farmyard. The father, an unfit man with crinkly hair and so many gold teeth his mouth looked like a brass fender, held his nose when one of the pigs approached. I was absolutely livid; *his* horrible aftershave was polluting our farmyard, and he had the cheek to hold his nose! His wife, picking her way across the mud in stiletto heels, kept saying, 'But the Tourist Board *recommended* you,' in puzzled tones. We never even met the children, who stayed in the car and screamed when they saw the dogs. Not our scene, as Marcus would have said.

We returned to our painting, tense and angry at first, but soon calmed by the rhythmic squish squish of the brushes. After a bit we started chuckling and mimicking our recent visitors and the game got so out of hand that by lunchtime we had decided to admit only those children whose parents complied with our new strict set of conditions. No Germans, or people with nylon shirts, deckle-edged paper or yellow eyelashes.

After lunch I popped out to check all was well on the animal front and found that Flicka, my favourite duck had hatched out some eggs.

'Brian, come quickly! Flicka's had ducklings.' Brian, followed by the dogs, hurried into the stable where Flicka had been brooding for some weeks. (She had got off to a false start by sitting on a clutch of coal nuts before we transferred her to duck eggs.) The dogs poked their noses under the stable door and Flicka hissed and spread her wings in alarm.

'How many?'

'I don't know, they keep moving. Aren't they sweet?' I picked one up and marvelled at the perfection of its tiny bill and delicate yellow overcoat.

'Twelve,' said Brian. 'Twelve out of fourteen, that's good going, Flicka, you're a clever girl.' Flicka let us pick her up and scratch her chin; she was the friendliest of the ducks and had often come into the house and tried to be promoted to dog, but her personal habits left so much to be desired we had not encouraged her.

'We can't stand here gushing all day,' said Brian. 'We've got De-horning and Castration this afternoon and we'll be late if we don't get ready.'

Getting ready only meant exchanging paint-stained jeans for dung-stained ones, and donning our third-best anoraks — fourth-best were for drains — and soon we were bowling along to the SHA member's place where the demonstration was being held. We hadn't any calves to de-horn or castrate, but we were so in love with the idea of becoming proper smallholders we went on every course going.

The instructor dealt with testicles first. We learnt that a Burdizzo castrator, used properly, is painless, leaving the calf with nothing more than a surprised look on its face. Then we were shown how to remove the horn buds with an electrically heated iron. The calves had to have two local anaesthetics for this as the base of the horn has a rich nerve supply, and while we were waiting for the xylotox to work we had a break and caught up on each others' news.

I said hullo to Betty, the goat and rabbit expert, and apologised for not finishing our chat about her stud buck.

'That's all right,' she said. 'Poor you, with those awful boys, I bet you gave them hell when you got them home.'

'We couldn't unfortunately — they were guests. Now, have you still got the buck and why are you selling him?'

'Hamish isn't really cut out to be a professional stud buck,' said Betty seriously. 'He's a romantic rabbit and I'm afraid I can't encourage romance in a commercial rabbitry.'

I stared at the wall and concentrated on keeping my cheek muscles under control. Thank goodness Brian was out of earshot. The idea of a buck whispering sweet nothings to the does instead of servicing them conveyor-belt fashion would have had him rolling on the floor.

'He came from a pet home,' Betty continued. 'And I think the children cuddled him a lot, he's awfully friendly.'

'Sounds just the job for us,' I said. 'What sort of litters does he father when he gets round to it?'

'Average ten a litter, there's nothing wrong with his fertility. I just feel he'd be happier with fewer does. Would you and Brian like to come to see him this afternoon when we've finished the calves? You haven't got to get back for milking, have you?'

'No, we had to have our cow put down. We'll be getting another one in the spring, but at the moment we're back with the milkman.'

'Oh, well, milkmen don't kick,' said Betty comfortingly.

We finished the calves and on the way over to Betty's I told Brian about Hamish.

'He's not the swashbuckling type,' I said. 'Not macho.'

And what, said Brian coldly, was the good of a buck that sat around in a Noel Coward smoking jacket making polite conversation? Ten minutes later he was sitting in Betty's kitchen drinking tea and sharing a biscuit with Hamish, who had a most amiable face and soft brown eyes.

'I thought New Zealands had red eyes,' I said.

'They do mainly,' said Betty. 'He may have some Californian in his ancestry — I haven't got his pedigree. Would you like to see the rest of the rabbits while you're here?'

The rabbits were housed in a long shed with sliding doors and air vents along the sides. The does with very young litters were in wooden hutches to ensure privacy, and then transferred to the main shed when their babies were older. The bucks were housed one to a cage to stop them fighting. Their does were brought to their cages for mating and removed afterwards. I could sympathise with Hamish for not being able to come to terms with this clinical set-up; a buck born to the life wouldn't mind, but a family pet would find it awfully boring.

We saw Betty's goats and calves and donkey which she had rescued via a donkey sanctuary. Vandals had done terrible things to the donkey, but under Betty's gentle care he was beginning to trust humans again. He allowed us to stroke his soft face and when we wandered back to the house we could see him resting his head on the stable door watching us.

'Talking of nutters, Betty,' I said. 'Who were those hippy youngsters at the AGM? The ones who were asking you about goats?'

'Oh them.' Betty sniffed. 'They sat through the meeting then decided not to join the SHA. They didn't really want to learn anything, that sort never do. They belong to one of those community set ups — you know, all high ideals and nobody washes up.'

'Are they still going?' Brian asked. 'I thought the flower people died out years ago. What do they live on?'

'The girl's got a rich daddy,' said Betty. 'He probably pays her to keep out of the house. She bought a goat from a friend of mine — I wouldn't sell her one — and the goat dried up because nobody remembered to milk it regularly. So now they're buying their yogurt in Sainsbury's and trying to get the goat in kid again.'

'I wish she'd spend some of daddy's allowance on soap,' I said. 'That toga thing she was wearing stank.' Brian looked at his watch.

'Come on, let's get Hamish home and have some supper.'

A sink full of dirty dishes greeted us when we got home, we'd been too busy painting and castrating to do it earlier. What was it Betty had said? 'All high ideals and nobody actually washes up.' I couldn't quite see Brian in a toga, though. Nor would there be time for high ideals until the bank started sending black statements instead of red ones.

Chapter Seven

THE EASTER HOLIDAYS span some five to six weeks what with State schools breaking up on different dates from private schools, and foreign schools having quite separate arrangements. By April, we were fully booked for the year, the bulk of the children coming from Britain, and the rest from France, Italy, America, Spain and Holland.

Addy, Brian's indefatigable mother, had offered to come for the Easter holidays. She would supervise the kitchen front, ensure that everything was shipshape when the health inspector dropped in, and generally keep us sane. With no Marcus or Sara on hand we decided to get two more helpers for Easter, and then an additional two for the long summer holiday.

Mandy came for a trial day in March. Her father, an acquaintance of Brian's, had briefed us beforehand:

'She's a grand little worker, but for God's sake don't let her answer the phone.' As his own telephone manner was curt to say the least, we were surprised, and he went on; 'There was a message on my phone pad the other day: "Dad, a man with a deep voice, coming 6 p.m. — bringing a collie." No name, no number to phone back, just that.'

'What's so terrible about that?' I asked. 'Your wife breeds dogs, doesn't she?'

'She breeds whippets, and anyway the message was for me. So I got home early for this mysterious man and his collie, and at six o'clock there he was on the doorstep with another man.'

'Where was the collie?'

'The other man was the collie. It was his *colleague*. That fool of a daughter of mine can't spell colleague.'

Brian and I looked at each other and burst out laughing. So other parents got scrambled phone messages too. We thought Marcus and Sara had the monopoly. Sara would jot down just key words, leaving us none the wiser, whereas Marcus would write a short novel in his elegant script, commenting on the emotional tone of the caller's voice, his probable occupation and size in shirts but often leaving out the nitty gritty of the message.

Mandy and I hit it off straight away. She was sixteen, waiting to be apprenticed to a National Hunt stables, and looked like a young Doris Day, even down to her gingham shirts. She had an inexhaustible supply of energy, a zany sense of humour and a mother who had won the Queen Elizabeth Cup, so in my book she got ten out of ten. Brian was dismayed at first to learn that horses were Mandy's *raison d'être*, but once he had seen how capable she was at everything she put her mind to, he admitted it was nice having her around. Coming from him, that meant ten out of ten too.

So Mandy started work, coming in just daily at first, as her home was only a fifteen-minute moped ride away, but promising to live in when the pace hotted up. Then Simon joined us, a very nice twenty-year-old, with tight curly hair like a Merino sheep.

'Handsome pair of youngsters,' observed Addy, watching them out of the kitchen window.

'Don't start matchmaking, Mum,' said Brian. 'They're here to work.'

We spent two days going over the premises inside and out to make sure everything was safe. The average age of the first twenty children was eight and you can bet your boots if there's a rotten branch in a tree or a wasps' nest in a chimney, an eight-year-old will find it.

All animals and poultry were wormed and their droppings burned. Simon and Brian donned protective clothing and moved a beehive to an out-of-bounds area next to the pansy crop. (Four months later, we found that the beehive had been empty all along.) Mandy and I set to with rubber curry combs and removed the ponies' winter coats, carefully saving the nitrogen-rich fur for the compost heap.

The four of us rehung a sagging gate, creosoted the poultry house, tightened wire fencing, cleaned out the garden pond and put sharp tools under lock and key. Mandy, for some extraordinary reason, put Brian's chainsaw in the larder. Addy regarded this as a reflection on her pastry and was not amused.

'Take it out, Mandy,' she said. 'Filthy greasy thing, it's dripping on to the shelf.'

'Sorry,' said Mandy, and lifted it on the draining board, where it formed a pool of oil.

'*Mandy*,' said Addy.

'Sorry,' said Mandy again. 'I'll go and ask Brian where he wants it.' Addy went upstairs to finish the bedrooms, and Mandy took the chainsaw out to Brian's shed. I picked up a cloth to wipe the draining board and found lots of black pellets sticking to it. Only when the tap had been running a few seconds did I realise that the pellets were Brian's precious sweetpea seeds which had been soaking on the cloth.

'*Mandy*,' I shouted out of the kitchen window. 'Stick your hand over the drain – *quick*.' Mandy shot over to the drain and capped her hand over the outlet pipe. So swift had been her response to my bizarre request that a major catastrophe was averted. I passed a colander out of the kitchen window.

'What are we playing?' Mandy asked.

'It's called stopping Brian having a coronary. Now, hold the colander under the outlet pipe and take your hand away. I'm going to run the tap slowly. Those black things are Brian's sweetpeas.'

'Oh *no*. How many?'

'Dozens and dozens. I doubt he's counted them, but he's bound to notice if half are missing.'

Slowly and carefully we retrieved the seeds. Some had collected in the U-bend, and we had to unscrew the huge nut to fish them out. Needless to say we flooded the kitchen floor.

'I make it 372,' said Mandy after several recounts. We arranged the seeds back on the cloth, mopped up the water on the floor, and made ourselves scarce before Hawkeye came in.

He didn't notice anything amiss until he came to plant the sweetpeas later in the day. By then Mandy and I had driven over to Betty's to collect a couple of orphan lambs – Betty was the SHA clearing house for sale and wanted animals and equipment – and had stayed chatting a while. When we got back, the lambs were the focus of attention and Brian's grumblings about being sold short measure by Suttons (he *had* counted them then) fell on conveniently deaf ears.

On Saturday, twenty children converged on us from all points of the compass – Italy, America, England and even Canvey Island.

'Strewth,' said Simon. 'The *noise*. Is it always like this?'

'They are a bit much,' I agreed. 'But you'll find that as long as they're noisy, everything's fine. It's the silences that unnerve me.' Simon banged the gong for supper and everyone streamed into the dining room and started spinning knives to find out who would marry whom and who had the ugliest face.

'Have you washed?' Mandy yelled above the din.

'Yes,' came the collective lie.

'When, last week?' Simon and Mandy shepherded the children upstairs and stood guard at the bottom. Suspiciously quickly the children clattered down again and held out their hands for inspection.

'Do you know what Daryl did, Mandy?' said one of the boys.

'No, what?'

'He washed the *backs* of his hands.' The other children gasped in horror.

'His dad's a doctor,' volunteered the informant. 'They all do that.'

'And dentists.'

'I like dentists, they have pink water.' Daryl's crime was generously overlooked in the heated dental debate that followed. Monica, a friendly eight-year-old chatterbox from Chester, staggered everyone when she told them that fairies in Cheshire pay fifteen pence for a milk tooth – far above the national average – while in Italy, according to Francesca, Anna and Sophia, teeth have no cash value.

After supper the children played outside while we washed up, and by eight o'clock they were in bed. One of the parents had given us a bottle of rosé and we were just settling down in the sitting room when the door opened and Daryl, the doctor's son, appeared. He turned out to be a nice, normal, eight-year-old American boy, with a pleasant dreamy nature. When he saw the bottle of rosé he came into the sitting-room and said

63

without preamble: 'If you guys are going to get mellow, I guess I'll join you.'

'You guess wrong, young sir,' Simon said. 'You're supposed to be in bed.' And he firmly marched Daryl upstairs again.

'Simon's very good with them, isn't he?' said Addy.

'M'm,' we agreed. Simon came down again and poked his head round the sitting-room door. 'I'm going to make Daryl some cocoa,' he said.

'Thanks, Simon. Sure you don't mind?'

Simon laughed. 'No, he's a nice kid, but he's used to being treated as an adult. He's never had to go to bed at eight before.' Addy tut tutted the way grandmothers do and we all waited to see if Daryl would come down again. Simon swore he hadn't put anything in the cocoa, but something must have done the trick because Daryl was asleep in minutes and for the rest of his holiday accepted eight o'clock bedtimes with no fuss.

A boy called Don was my flavour of the week though. He was a bookworm. His parents, as stupid as their car danglies, had 'warned' us that Don would 'always have his nose in a book unless you stop him' and when I had taken him to the playroom to show him the books, he had nearly cried with pleasure. His face had gone quite red as he ran his hands along the spines of the hardbacks.

'So *many*,' he kept saying. 'Are they all yours?'

'Brian's and mine from when we were children and our children's added to them. These in the playroom are all children's books, but if you want something harder ours are in here.' I opened our sitting-room door and you would have thought I was showing him into the Bodleian from the look on his face. Not that our collection is anything spectacular, but to a child from a bookless home it must have seemed a land of milk and honey.

'I'm here for two weeks,' he said excitedly. 'How many free periods can I have for reading?'

'You're on holiday, Don. It's all free periods as you call it. You can read all day if you want to.'

Which is just what he did for almost the whole of his fortnight. Not that he was a recluse — far from it — but directly

64

he got back from a riding, river or seaside expedition he would
grab his current book and disappear.

'He's got advanced tastes for an eight-year-old,' Addy said
one day. 'I'm sure Brian wasn't reading John Buchan at eight.'

'I should think his reading age is twelve plus,' I said. 'He's
read *Coral Island* and two Arthur Ransomes in three days.
Have you seen the way he takes the jackets off the hardbacks
and sniffs them? I can remember doing that at his age with
new books but ours are so old now I wouldn't have thought
they still smelled nice.'

'He's a sweet boy,' said Addy. 'Surprising really coming
from those horrible parents. Perhaps he's adopted.' Addy likes
to think that children's sterling qualities are inherited. 'What
I can't understand,' she went on, 'is how he can possibly be as
book starved as he makes out. Surely he's got a library to go
to?'

'He says his parents only let him go once a week and he can
only have two books on one ticket, so by Monday he's finished
them.'

Don's favourite quiet place was on top of the stored hay in
one of the barns. He took a dozen books and arranged them
along one of the rafters using bricks for bookends. With biscuits and chocolates scrounged from Addy, he would settle
down in his hay nest and read until the sun moved off the
skylight. If he had been a cat, he would have purred.

The first week passed in a flash. Nobody quarrelled or grizzled
or got homesick and the sun shone nearly every day. We
bought a fifth pony through Tony the farrier and fount of all
local knowledge, and called him Owen.

'He'll do you for the season,' Tony said as he unloaded the
eleven-hand grey from the horse box.

'Aah,' said the children, and crowded round Owen patting
and stroking him.

'What do you mean "for the season"?' I said, 'Is he old?'

'No,' said Tony.

'Unfit?'

'No.'

'Vices?'

'No.'

'Oh, for heaven's sake Tony, stop saying no. What's wrong with him?'

'Nothing. Only you won't want to keep him. He won't fit in here. You'll see.' Just then Tony caught sight of Hamish the rabbit, fast asleep in the arms of one of the little Italian girls. Hamish was dressed in a pink doll's dress and his claws had been painted with felt pen the same shade of pink.

'Good God almighty, what's that?' said Tony, peering in amazement at Hamish's outfit.

'That's Hamish. He's our new stud buck.' Tony sucked in his cheeks and busied himself fastening the back of the lorry.

'He's laughing,' Mandy said.

'No, no, not me Mandy,' Tony's lips twitched. 'If my old dad was alive today he'd say —'

'*Tony*,' I cut in quickly. With forty small ears flapping I felt we could do without the indelicate pronouncements of Tony's old dad. 'Not in front of the children.'

'My parents say it in French,' piped up a small boy called Greg.

'So do mine,' agreed another. '*Pas devant les enfants* they say.'

'I can speak French,' offered Francesca, the eldest Italian girl.

'Don't *tell* them silly,' said Denise. 'They won't do it if you tell them.'

'See what you've started, Tony,' I said.

'What I've started?' protested Tony. 'All I was going to say is I've never seen a working stud in a pink frock before.' He sucked his cheeks in again. 'Does he, er, have to get dressed up before he. . .?'

'Can we get back to the pony please. There's nothing wrong with him, but we won't want to keep him. Right?'

'Right.' Tony swung himself into the driving cab. 'One thing I'll tell you — you won't get *him* into a pink frock.'

Tony had summed up Owen in a nutshell. We had had him only a few days when we realised that poor Owen was Eeyore personified — he felt life had dealt him a weak hand, while everyone else had aces. He worked hard, unmotivated by praise

66

or reward. Life was work, wasn't it? No, you needn't bother giving me polos or carrots, save them for a more deserving pony. This mild paranoia is all very well for a stuffed toy, but in a flesh and blood animal it is not endearing.

'I think he's thick,' Mandy said one day as we tacked up the ponies for the children's rides. One of the small girls had put Owen's bridle on him incorrectly, and whereas any normal pony would have taken it off and probably trodden on it to make the point, Owen had put up with it in martyred silence. Mandy removed it and put it back on properly.

'There you are, little feller,' she said cheerily. 'That feels better, doesn't it?' No response, no flick of the ears or nuzzling of pockets.

'Perhaps he's deaf.'

'No, I thought of that,' said Mandy. 'He's too obedient to the voice to be deaf.'

'I wish I was deaf sometimes,' said Simon coming in to the yard with half a dozen children in tow.

We got the first five riders mounted and set out for a two hour leading-rein session. Brian went in front leading Noah, followed by Simon and Monty, then Wellington off the lead as his rider was semi-competent. I went next with tiny Rocky and Mandy with Owen brought up the rear. The fifteen other children followed on foot saying every few minutes 'Is it my turn yet?' and 'I'm sure that's more than half an hour.'

Every half hour we stopped and changed the riders over. If we were lucky the children would be happy just being led at a walk, but usually our little slave drivers would demand 'more trotting please' and we would summon up some energy and run with the ponies until whoever was leading slowed down. As a slimming regime it beats dieting any day – you can stuff yourself full of chocolate biscuits and still lose half a stone a week.

'Heels down, Sophia, and elbows in. Sit up straight, Greg. Very good, Monica, but shorten your reins a bit.' Mandy was a born teacher and could instruct five at a time with no trouble. I had problems *breathing* let alone instructing and made several appeals to the others to have some of the rides conducted in the circle at home.

67

'Don't you understand?' Brian said for the umpteenth time, 'If each child has a half-hour ride and we're leading them, we have to walk the same distance whether it's in the circle or round the lanes. Do you see?' There was so much sweat in my eyes I was beyond seeing anything. I could understand Brian's geometry in theory but it didn't *seem* so long in the circle.

'Besides it's boring for the ponies doing circle work.' Mandy sided with Brian; so did Simon who had yards of leg and liked long walks.

'You wait till you have your day off, Mandy,' I threatened. 'This lot will do two hours in the circle and like it.'

'Bri. . . yern,' wailed Monica, the girl from Cheshire where the rich tooth fairies came from. 'Noah's eaten my posy — my *best* bunch — I wanted to save it to show Mummy.'

'What was in it?' said Mandy and I simultaneously.

'Primroses and violets and four sorts of grasses.'

'That's OK,' Mandy grinned. 'Nothing to harm Noah in that.'

'Can we stop so I can pick some more flowers?'

'Yes,' I said eagerly and Brian said no at the same time. The ayes had it and we stopped for a breather while the children picked primroses which cascaded down the banks in their thousands. Violets too grew in abundance and not the shrinking sort either. These were bold firm blooms on sturdy stems which as ex-florists we could appreciate as something special.

'Come on, horribles,' said Brian looking at his watch. 'Honda and Suzuki will be wanting their lunchtime bottles.' The last five children clambered aboard the grazing ponies and tugged ineffectually at the reins.

'*Legs*,' Mandy and I roared in unison. The children dug wellington-clad heels into the ponies' fat stomachs and the procession moved off, gathering momentum when the ponies realised they were going home.

The lambs, Honda and Suzuki (by request of Marcus), were on five feeds a day — 8 a.m., 12 noon, 4 p.m., 8 p.m., and midnight. The children took turns to give them all but the night feed and by some sort of telepathic arrangement among themselves always seemed to know whose turn it was. If we were late back from the rides, we would hear Honda and

Suzuki complaining loudly in their piercing trebles as soon as we reached home.

All too soon Friday came around. Six children were staying on for the second week, so there were only fourteen suitcases to pack and two million wellingtons and sandals to identify. Saturday left us shattered what with seeing departures off, changing the beds and welcoming new arrivals.

By 10 p.m. all the children were asleep, Addy had gone up for an early night and Simon was in the bath. Brian and I were licking our wounds over a cup of cocoa when the phone rang.

'Oh *no*,' Brian groaned.

'I'll get it,' I said. It was Mrs Hamilton, mother of six-year-old Greg who had gone home that morning.

'I'm sorry to trouble you so late,' she said. 'But I can't get Greg to sleep. He's left his teddy-bear there and he's crying his eyes out. I know there's nothing you can do tonight, but I wonder if you'd have a word with Greg just to let him know you'll post it on?'

'Of course,' I said. 'Hullo Greg, you're up late, aren't you?' Greg swallowed his sobs and said hoarsely, 'I want Teddy.'

'Teddy's asleep, Greg. Asleep in Parsley's basket,' I improvised. 'All tucked up warm next to Parsley. Parsley's looking after him.' I wondered how long I could keep this up especially as I could see Brian beginning to laugh.

'Could I speak to Teddy please?' Greg's voice was wavery. 'I'm lonely.'

'Yes, Greg, yes. I'll go and wake him up.' This would wipe the smirk off Brian's face. I put my hand over the mouthpiece. 'Brian, listen. You — are — a — teddy-bear,' I said in a stage whisper.

'*What?*' said Brian in horror. 'Oh no, I couldn't. Where's Simon?'

'Having a bath. Come on it's easy. You're a tired teddy-bear and you've been in Parsley's basket.' Brian glared like a laser beam and took the phone from me.

'Hullo Greg,' he said, in a deep growly voice.

'Not so *sinister*,' I whispered. 'His mother's trying to get him to bed.'

'Shut up. Who's doing this?' Brian mouthed, and returned

69

to his growly voice. 'You woke me up, Greg. I was asleep in Parsely's basket. Ho ho ho,' he added for good measure, sounding more like a bad Father Christmas than a teddy-bear. Greg must have said something then for Brian continued: 'Oh no Greg, I wasn't lost, I was hiding. I'm having an extra day's holiday here. I'm very tired though, so tired — aah aah,' he yawned theatrically, then realised it was wasted down the phone and reverted to plain deep and growly. 'I'm coming home tomorrow.'

'It's Sunday tomorrow — no post.' I rolled round on the floor and stuffed my hanky in my mouth. Simon came in, in pyjamas and dressing-gown. Brian was saying, 'Two days' extra holiday — what a lucky Teddy I am. Ho ho ho.'

'What's wrong with his throat?' Simon asked. 'And what's all the ho hoing?'

'He's being a teddy-bear.'

Simon grinned: 'I wish we had a tape recorder.'

Teddy eventually managed to say good-night and with many kisses blown down the phone, rang off. Simon and I immediately started: 'If-you-go-down-in-the-woods-today . . .'

'Don't start,' said Brian warningly. 'We Teds can get very violent if we're pushed. Is there any cocoa left?'

'Yes. Is your throat sore?'

'My *squeaker*,' Brian corrected. 'We have squeakers, not throats.'

Chapter Eight

PEOPLE OFTEN USED to say to us, 'What do you *do* with yourselves so far from civilisation?' as though we had to hack a path
through virgin jungle in order to get to shops, libraries,
dentists, etc.

Since leaving London to 'bury' ourselves in the backwoods of
one of the busiest tourist counties in Britain, the only amenity
we missed was a good big library. The small town libraries
were as good as funds allowed and the staff did miracles with
their scandalously small amounts of money, but after London
it was irksome to have to go on a waiting list for new books.

As to what we did, well the same as most people do – work,
eat and play. Our working day consisted of tending our farm
stock, domestic pets, crops and guests, and our leisure time
was taken up with hobbies and visiting our rapidly growing
number of friends. This was more or less how we had lived in
London since the advent of decimalisation and VAT had put
theatres and restaurants beyond our means, and shopping had
never had any appeal anyway.

A typical day when there were no children staying would
start at dawn – anything from 5 a.m. to 7 a.m. depending on
the time of year – with animal feeds and milking. By about
9 a.m., we would be ready for a huge breakfast and gallons of
tea, and over breakfast we would sort out the post, spiking
anything that could wait and putting the rest in a pile at the
end of the table.

After breakfast, Brian would go to work in the vegetable
garden and I would run a hoover over the bits that showed, see
to the post, then go outside to muck out the animals. A quick
snack for lunch – soup, bread and cheese and fruit – then more
outdoor work, maybe a bonfire or renovating an outhouse,
weeding or chopping wood.

If there was a farm sale near by, we would always try and go to it in the hope of picking up a bargain. After we joined the Smallholders' Association, we could be sure of seeing someone we knew at farm sales, and we would egg each other on to buy prehistoric machinery or job lots of junk. Our pony minding friends, Rob and Chris, once made a serviceable pair of gates out of two iron bedsteads, bought in a sale. Not being inventive ourselves, we were always mystified when we saw our fellow smallholders snapping up empty oil drums or bits of tin and then consumed with envy when we visited their homes and found this junk turned into heat exchangers or granny annexes.

Back home for evening milking and feeds — animal and selves — then a few hours free to read or watch television or see friends, then the final check on poultry house doors before bed.

When there were children staying they helped with whatever took their fancy — grooming ponies, cleaning out rabbit hutches, hosing the yard or delousing the pigs. There is nothing quite as enthusiastic or so inefficient as your average seven-year-old and all the chores took twice as long when they helped.

During the second week of the Easter holidays, we had to bonfire fourteen churns of spoiled butter. Brian had contracted with a local dairy to take away all their outdated produce as we could use the milk powder for the pigs and burn the rest. Up to that time the small amounts of cheesey waste that we collected weekly was easily disposed of by burying it in the compost or by burning.

The huge amount of butter we had to get rid of this time was rancid and packed down so hard in the narrow-necked ten-gallon churns it was difficult to get out. We built a huge bonfire from hacked down blackberry bushes, then rolled the churns up to the pile and instructed the children to start excavating. Armed with metal spoons and pieces of flat wood they dug away merrily at the butter, flinging the yellow gobs on to the unlit fire and shrieking with laughter as the butter landed accidentally on purpose on someone's head. Then they struck a snag.

The churns were about three feet high and the children couldn't reach more than halfway down even with their spoons. Also they were so plastered with grease we couldn't risk lighting the fire until they were less combustible.

'I'll finish getting the butter out if you'll clean the kids,' Brian offered, and Addy, Simon, Mandy and I accepted as it seemed we had the easier job. Twenty children later we weren't quite so sure. We filled both baths with hot water and washing-up liquid and put the children in two at a time, like sheep in a dip, dunking their heads right under to get all the butter out of their hair.

Addy and I did ten, and Simon and Mandy the other ten. Having a combined sixty years practice at bathing children, we finished first and popped into the other bathroom to see if they needed a hand. It was like a sauna in there with pink bodies everywhere.

'I think your water's a bit hot,' said Addy, feeling it with her hand. 'You should test it before they get in.'

'No, that's OK,' said Mandy airily. 'If they turn blue we know it's too cold, and if it's too hot they turn red.' I liked this litmus paper approach, but Addy tutted and said: 'Poor little things, let me finish them for you.'

'No, we can manage thanks, we'll be down in a sec. Hoy, you − get your pants off.' This was to a modest six-year-old clutching his towel round his waist. 'I didn't say you had got butter on your willy,' Mandy went on, 'but you're not getting in the bath with your pants on.' Addy and I retreated.

The butter bonfire was spectacular with flames reaching nearly to the telephone wires some thirty feet above. It went on and on and we hadn't the heart to put the children to bed while it was still crackling excitingly. It was pitch dark before it had died down and the little ones were yawning their heads off. We gave them marshmallows to toast in the fire on the end of long sticks and they managed to cover themselves with charcoal goo so that we had to wash them all over again.

They were a mixed bunch that week and we never did discover who it was who started the catch-word 'suffer' (pronounced *suff*-er with the emphasis on the first syllable). It was irritating at first and then infuriating. You would be quietly going about your business when suddenly out of nowhere two or three small children would pop up with their arms stretched out stiffly in front like sleepwalkers and their fingers splayed rigidly. '*Suff*-er,' they would intone, pointing their fingers (ray-guns?) straight at your eyes. I don't know why we found it so irritating — after all, everyone is used to the 'bang bang you're dead' routine with two fingers — but we all hated it and administered thick ears all round if we could catch the tormentors.

'I expect Miles started it,' said Brian rather unfairly. Brian didn't like Miles, well none of us did really, but Brian is more intolerant than most about bad manners.

Poor Miles, it was hardly his fault that he had no manners — his parents were the ultra-progressive type — but it made looking after him more a battle than a pleasure. He arrived wearing a T-shirt advertising the fact that he was a Friend of the Earth (he was also on pretty intimate terms with egg yolk and felt pen judging by the state of his face), and being a Friend of the Earth apparently necessitated being an enemy of soap and water.

Washing before meals was one of the few rules that we enforced; a *laissez-faire* attitude to farmyard bacteria simply isn't on when you're in charge of other people's children. So, what with eight-year-old Miles having to be forcibly scrubbed three times a day, and not knowing when the *suff*-er game would break out, we abandoned any hopes we may have had that the new intake would be as little trouble as the last.

We were right. An adenoidal six-year-old called Carol absentmindedly removed several square yards of wallpaper from her bedroom wall one night. She was sharing a small double room with her five-year-old brother Robert and the two of them had lain in their bunks picking away at the wall until Carol's section was down to the plaster. Robert's fingers were not as nimble as Carol's and his place only needed repasting.

'Bandy shouted at me,' Carol wept.

'Serves you right,' I said. 'And shut up.' Earth Mother always turns nasty when people snivel. 'Pick up that brush and paste the wall where the paper's torn.' I cut a fresh piece of wallpaper from the spare roll left over from redecorating and waited impatiently while Carol pasted the wall. Then together we placed the patch over the damaged area and I showed Carol how to jiggle the paper until the pattern matched the adjacent piece.

'It's dice, very pretty,' said Carol. I patted the airholes out with a clean rag.

'There, all done. It won't be dry until tomorrow, so *don't* touch it. OK?'

Next morning the wallpaper was shredded all over the floor like confetti. Carol, oblivious of my mounting blood pressure, was in the yard waiting for the ponies to be tacked up. Seizing her by her anorak collar I started to march her back to the house and on the way we collided with Brian coming out of the tack room holding Miles by *his* anorak collar.

'Snap,' I said, letting go of Carol. 'What's *your* problem?'

'Young Friend of the Earth here,' said Brian, jerking his head towards Miles, 'refuses to wear a riding hat.'

'I keep telling him,' said Miles, 'but he won't listen. I keep telling him, I'm inclined to get claustrophobia in a hat.'

'Well, in that case, we'll be inclined to leave you behind when we go riding,' I said.

'That's what *he* said,' said Miles sulkily. Carol sensed that the heat was off her for a moment and slipped into the tack room. She came out again wearing a riding hat.

'I'll have Biles's turn,' she said. 'Can I ride Rocky, please?' I let her go and went back to the house with Brian and Miles.

'Could you keep an eye on Miles for a couple of hours, please Mum?' said Brian. 'He's not going riding today,' Miles looked flabbergasted when he realised we meant what we said. By arguing about not wearing a hat he had unwittingly touched on a very raw nerve indeed.

When we got back from the rides Addy and Miles were best of friends. Truby King and Dr Spock certainly saw eye to eye when it came to rolling out gingerbread men.

Quentin was another boy who etched himself on our memories. He was what, in some parts of Devon, they call a 'tacker', meaning an afterthought or late arrival. He had four sisters, the youngest fifteen when he was born, and had spent a cocooned infanthood because all the females in the family considered him delicate.

His mother, one of those limp handshakers who always

make me want to give them a shot of calcium, handed me a notebook containing a not very potted medical history of Quentin. It started at day ten with a four-ounce bowel movement, and ended six days ago when the now eight-year-old had complained of leg pains.

'We were in two minds whether to let him come at all,' his mother said, after I had flipped through the epic story of Quentin's measles, earaches and constipation. 'But then we told ourselves he must learn to stand on his own two feet.' I looked at her to see if she was being intentionally funny with all these twos, but she was so earnest I had to sit firmly on the giggle that was threatening to erupt.

'But what exactly is the problem, Mrs Pearce? Doesn't Quentin want to come?'

'Oh yes, he does. He saw it on the telly and made us write away for your brochure. It was his idea really – his daddy and I wouldn't have thought of sending such a mite away on his own.' The mite in question smiled at me knowingly and in a flash I got the picture. Quentin was outgrowing his loving, crushing, fusspot parents.

'We sent away for one or two other brochures,' Mrs Pearce went on. 'But the Tourist Board recommended you.' (We often wondered just who our guardian angel was at the British Tourist Board.) 'And as you're a mother yourself you're bound to understand about his, er, special needs.' She raised her eyebrows questioningly and I thought, Oh God, she's another laxative freak. Quite a few mothers put a packet of laxatives in with the children's clothes and we used to cut out the middleman by putting them straight in the dustbin.

'What needs?'

'Well, he must go to bed early. A growing boy needs at least twelve hours sleep.'

'Oh at least,' I agreed, perhaps a shade too eagerly. 'What else?'

What it boiled down to was that Mrs Pearce wanted Quentin to get the same hothouse treatment he was accustomed to at home: crusts off his bread, his bed made for him, and various substances dropped into the appropriate hole if he complained of earache, sore throat or stuffed-up nose.

'And could you keep the notebook up to date, please? Just jot down any little upsets he may get. It helps the doctor, you see.'

Looking through Mrs Pearce's notebook later in the evening we all agreed that Quentin's GP must have wished he had opted for deep-sea diving instead of medicine. There was obviously nothing wrong with the child that a new mother wouldn't put right.

'Listen to this,' Mandy said. 'Doctor says nothing to worry about. Then a week later: Doctor says Quentin not allergic to Elastoplast. That's the fifth thing he's not allergic to. And they *weighed* his nappies when he was a baby — can you imagine? It says here — '4 oz passed' — that was when he was ten days old. It seems a lot, doesn't it?'

Simon said we'd need a new septic tank if Quentin's output was still relative to his body weight. This brought the house down and Mandy, rather to Addy's disapproval, nicknamed Quentin Supershit.

Quentin very quickly learned to stand on his own two feet. Simon and Mandy made sure that he didn't slow down the pace of the day, by simply ignoring his cries of 'Wait for me *please*' as he struggled to keep up with the others. We removed three of his five layers of clothing, but he found even putting on a T-shirt and pullover took far longer than anyone else because he had never had to do it.

Although he was a bit of a drip we had to admire his courage. He was dunked in the icy river, left stranded up a tree, sacrificed by Red Indians and accidentally branded by the same Red Indians with a hot marshmallow. For the first day he cried with frustration but, as crying got him nowhere, took to bellowing with fury at each new indignity. 'I hate you all,' he would roar. 'I wish I hadn't come to this horrible holiday.' To everyone's surprise and at his own request he was booked in for a further week in the summer holiday.

My birthday coincided with Badminton that year, and I was going to have a day off instead of all those boring old cashmere sweaters and diamond tiaras.

The coach taking us to Badminton had been booked by a local riding club of which Ursula was a member. 'Come as my guest,' she'd said. 'I'll treat you.' And what a treat it was, bowling along in the company of adults only, what a treat to know that their bladders and bowels were their own responsibility. No 'Ten Green Bottles' or 'One Man Went to Mow'. Bliss.

'This is heaven,' I said to Ursula as the coach sped past fields of leaping lambs and unfolding greenery.

'Marvellous,' Ursula agreed. 'What a lot of catkins there are this year, aren't there? By the way, I thought you said Mandy was coming? I don't see her on the coach.'

'She's going with friends, we'll probably see her there.'

'So Brian and his mother and Simon are holding the fort?'

'They'll manage. They won't have to do the rides today, we told the kids the ponies needed a rest day.'

It was perishing cold at Badminton and rained on and off all day but we had a lovely time. All the big names in the horse world were there and the air tingled with excitement as the magnificently fit horses galloped round the course, flinging up mud in their wake.

There were marquees too, with stalls selling everything from insurance to hoof picks. Ursula bought me a dainty little pencil sketch of a mare and foal and as we were leaving the tent we banged into Mandy coming in to shelter from the rain.

'Hi,' she said, shaking the water from her coat and soaking us. 'Enjoying it?'

'You bet. How long have you been here?'

'We came early to get a good parking place for the Land Rover. We've been sitting on the roof – I'm wet through,' she added unnecessarily.

Then she told us how her friend's labrador had disgraced himself. He slipped his lead and made a beeline for the Queen whose party was parked near by. He jumped up at the Queen and left muddy paw prints all down her coat. Mandy's friend, scarlet with embarrassment and expecting to be sent to the Tower, hauled her dog away and apologised.

'The Queen was super,' Mandy concluded. 'She's a real doggy person.'

'Have a nice day?' asked Addy, putting the kettle on.

'Super, thanks. How about you?'

'It could have been worse. It's been raining nearly all day so they've been indoors a lot. Simon took them for a walk, then they had a picnic in the hay barn only the picnic turned into a hay fight.'

'It always does. Didn't Don mind them invading his reading room?'

No, it seemed Don didn't, for the simple reason that clever Don had wheedled Addy into lighting a nice log fire for him in our sitting room. And the strange thing was that none of the other children had minded this preferential treatment. None of them could see the attraction of spending a day buried in a book when there were games to be played, friends to be fought and television to be watched.

Brian came in with an assortment of chocolate-coated children clinging to him. They had been feeding the teatime scraps to the piglets, I was informed by each child separately, and had I seen Mark Phillips at Badminton?

'No, I didn't see Mark Phillips,' I said. 'Have you been good? You had chocolate spread for tea, didn't you?'

'Ooh, aren't you clever, how did you know?'

Two of the small girls started a heated debate on whether Mark Phillips or Denise's grandad had the most handsome face, and I was saved from having to arbitrate on this one as Brian said, 'By the way, there's a shovel for you. It came by post.'

'A shovel?' Not a cashmere sweater or diamond tiara then. It was a nice shovel as shovels go, with a sturdy wooden handle and a black painted business end. 'Happy Birthday. Love Sara,' it said on the card, so I phoned her in London.

'Thanks for the shovel, Sara.'

'Oh good, it arrived safely. Sorry I couldn't get a rake, they said in the hardware shop they'd never heard of a muck rake.'

'A *muck* rake?'

'You sound like Lady Bracknell,' Sara giggled. 'Marcus said you wanted a muck rake.'

'He should get some of that hair out of his ears, I don't know anything about a muck rake.'

'I've got a list here. Bath oil, it says, and yellow string gloves and a muck rake and — '

The penny dropped. 'Mug rack,' I interrupted. 'I said I wanted a mug rack. For the kitchen.'

'Oh.'

'But I'd much rather have the shovel. Really I would. It must have cost a fortune though.'

'M'm, it was expensive. I sold a pair of jeans to get it.'

It seemed there was a shop in Oxford Street that paid good money for secondhand jeans, the older the better. 'If they're faded *and* patched you can get more than you paid for them new,' Sara explained. 'It's the in thing to be patched all over.'

We rang off and I went to tell Brian that for the first time in our lives our wardrobes were the height of fashion.

Changeover Saturday, a merciful blur now. I remember having to pacify Miles's mother because Miles was too clean, and Quentin's mother because Quentin now wore two layers of clothing instead of five. And then there was the seven-year-old girl — the one with the grandad who looked like Mark Phillips — who gave her mother a blow by blow account of a small operation I had carried out on the kitchen table a few days previously.

'Michael had something stuck in his ear, Mummy, so Faith put him on the kitchen table to have a look.'

'Did she, dear?'

'Yes. On the kitchen *table*, Mummy. Michael was awfully good, it was a hayseed or something and Faith put olive oil down his ear with a warm teaspoon.'

'And did the hayseed come out?'

'Yes, only it took ages. Faith cleaned both his ears with Q-tips.'

'I use Q-tips — they're very gentle, aren't they?' said the mother. I nodded dumbly and felt my face getting that embalmed look.

'And then she put cottonwool on tweezers and got lots of wax out of his ears.'

'Ugh, *darling* must you? Have you had a lovely holiday? Did you go riding?'

'Mummy, let me finish telling you about Michael.'

I racked my brains to think of a way to get this lot safely off the premises before Mummy cottoned on to the fact that Michael was one of the pigs.

Chapter Nine

THE WEATHER WAS normal for April – cold, wet and windy. After the drought in the previous year we would never again grumble about rain and indeed we still welcomed each rainy day because it meant the reservoir was filling up. The cold though was quite another kettle of fish.

It delayed the growth of the spring grass so that grazing had to be rationed and grumbling ponies confined to the yard and fed on hay. It made seaside outings little short of torture what with having to revive mauve-lipped children after swimming, and having to carry enough hot drinks for everyone right down to the beach. Worst of all, it meant that there were even more clothes to keep track of. Normally the children would have worn shorts, sandals and T-shirts with a sweater in the evenings, but add to that an anorak apiece, extra sweaters, scarves and even gloves and you find a lot of the day is taken up with reuniting garments with their owners.

But suddenly one day winter turned to summer and caught us on the hop. We chopped the legs off our jeans, threw our heavy sweaters into the linen basket and rushed outside to expose as much skin as possible to the sun before it changed its mind.

The yard looked like the spring scene in *Seven Brides for Seven Brothers* with ducklings and chicks taking dust baths in the sunshine and all the other creatures grunting or clucking or bleating in astonishment at this new hot yellow stuff falling out of the sky.

The rabbits and guinea pigs were released from their winter hutches into outdoor pens and the children were entranced at the way they first sniffed the grass suspiciously, then, as the day progressed, explored more and more of their new world. The baby rabbits – Hamish's three-week-old children –

hopped prettily to the wire mesh where the group of kids were kneeling watching them. At the least movement from outside their mother thumped the ground with her hind legs and the babies shot back to her side.

The grass grew almost visibly and after a week we decided there was enough to support a cow as well as the five ponies. We had not intended to be cowless for so long and had put the word round the smallholders' grapevine that we were looking for a Jersey heifer. Thanks to the courses and farm visits we had had through the SHA, we now had enough practical experience of looking at cows to be able to pick out exactly what we wanted.

She was a beautiful heifer, two years old, with a birth certificate to prove it, and in calf to a pedigree Jersey. She had a good coat, enormous expressive dark eyes and a well-shaped plump udder. We called her Elizabeth Taylor.

Parsley, not wishing to be upstaged by this aristocratic newcomer, quietly and efficiently gave birth to her second litter of puppies, another five — three girls and two boys — and when these were two weeks old we had a phone call from the collie breeder saying that our collie pup was ten weeks old and ready for collection.

By this time there was only one child staying — a likeable ten-year-old boy called Daniel. He was from Venezuela and his parents were in England for a week on business which they felt was dull for Daniel so they sent him to us. Daniel spoke virtually no English but as his main passion in life was animals we had little trouble communicating. He came with us to collect the puppy and comforted her all the way home with South American endearments.

The puppy's pedigree and physical condition were faultless but being kennel-reared she was socially backward. She had never encountered a hoover or a telephone or a flushing lavatory and the noises these made sent her scurrying into her basket for weeks after we had her. She would have liked Parsley to adopt her and tried several times to climb in with the younger puppies but Parsley naturally misunderstood her intentions and drove her back to her own basket. Honey was friendly enough but has never been over-maternal and refused point blank to let the pupply sleep next to her.

We named her Ella on account of her strong singing voice. Even when she was still a tiny pup she would sit back on her haunches and, making her mouth into an O, would sing straight up into the air. She looked like a scruffy little wolf and we couldn't imagine her growing into an elegant 'Lassie' dog.

Daniel loved her and the two lambs equally. The four of them had a wonderful time in the garden playing chasing games and sometimes football. Ella didn't have any sheepdog instincts and was quite happy to let the lambs do all the chasing, then when she was tired she would fall asleep on Daniel's lap and let him protect her from the exuberant Honda and Suzuki.

Addy went home for a well-earned rest and Simon left to join a group of friends who were hitch-hiking to Turkey. Mandy came in most days for a few hours and Brian and I were able to go to most of the SHA courses and lectures. We learned a little about a lot of things – teazle growing, beekeeping, skin care (sheep and rabbit skins, not human), pig husbandry, pheasant rearing and manures – and booked ourselves in for a comprehensive animal-husbandry course which the Association had planned for the autumn.

One day Daniel ran indoors and started to mime giving birth. The commentary was in Venezuelan but birth is unmistakably birth in any language. We kidded him that we couldn't understand him. Brian said: 'Have you got piles, Daniel?' and Mandy fetched a chamber pot, which sent Daniel into fits of laughter.

'Come,' he said, still giggling helplessly, and led the way to the pigs' enclosure. There was Rose Hip, the Gloucester Old Spot gilt, busily producing her first litter. Daniel said proudly, 'Bebby,' and pointed to the three piglets.

'Piglets, Daniel. They're called piglets.'

'Bebby pig-lets?'

'Yes, all right, baby piglets.'

'More?' he asked. We all nodded firmly and Brian said, 'There'd better be.' Rose Hip had been sent to a pedigree boar for a stud fee of twenty pounds.

Daniel settled down happily on the grass. 'I stay,' he said.

We all stayed and saw Rose Hip safely delivered of five strapping daughters and two sons. It was as much fun seeing Daniel enchanted by the births as watching the process itself. Just before the afterbirth came away Brian remembered some urgent work that needed doing elsewhere and wondered if he had better take Daniel too.

'No, let him stay,' Mandy said confidently. 'We'll explain.'

A sow's afterbirth is massive; it more than fills a two-gallon bucket, and Daniel's eyes widened in alarm as I picked up the steaming blubbery mass and slopped it into the bucket Mandy was holding.

'Is dead?' he asked.

'No. Is finished,' I said ungrammatically. 'Er, this is, er baby piglets' food.' I pointed at my mouth. Daniel looked puzzled and shrugged his shoulders.

'He doesn't understand,' Mandy said. 'He thinks you mean food — like fish and chips.'

If there are any strange tales about birds and bees going round the school playgrounds of Venezuela I expect they originated from Daniel's biology lesson that day.

After Mandy and I had made Rose Hip comfortable and settled each piglet on to a teat, we went indoors and tried to explain birth in pidgin English. Daniel got gigglier and gigglier — plainly he thought we were mad.

'It's no good,' said Mandy. 'We'll have to draw it.'

'Can you draw?'

'No, can you?'

'No, worse luck. I'll have a go though.' I drew a balloon and inside the balloon a cup of tea and a plate with a knife and fork. 'What's this, Daniel?' I said, pushing the paper across the table. He looked at it for a moment.

'Hotel?' he guessed.

'*Food*, you South American cretin,' said Mandy, snatching the paper away. She scribbled some food on to the empty plate and some steam coming out of the cup. 'There, food. Do you see?'

'Food,' said Daniel obediently.

'Now watch carefully,' I said, and drew a pig underneath the balloon. Mandy said it looked more like a hippo but I told her to shut up in case we confused him. I drew seven little pigs inside the main pig and held up the paper.

'Bebby pig-lets,' said Daniel. I hugged him for recognising talent when he saw it.

'Now for the difficult bit,' said Mandy. 'How are you going to get the food to the piglets?'

'I don't know.'

'Let me have a go.' Mandy picked up a red felt tip.

'Don't make it too graphic,' I said, taking the red away and handing her a blue.

'Not blue, it could mean oxygen starvation.' She picked up a green and drew a wiggly hosepipe to represent the umbilical cord from the balloon with the food to the seven piglets. She branched the hose into the seven mouths making it look as though the piglets were blowing up the food balloon. 'Do you understand, Daniel?' She pointed to the drawing.

'No,' said Daniel, smiling broadly.

'I think he's having us on,' I said. I brought the bucketful of afterbirth into the kitchen. 'Food,' I said.

'Food.' Daniel nodded doubtfully. I put my finger on the drawing. 'Food – hotel – OK?'

'Food. OK.'

'And this?' indicating the pregnant pig drawing.

'Bebby piglets.'

'Good. Piglets eat food. OK?'

'OK.' Daniel pulled a fresh sheet of paper towards him and drew a very recognisable pig.

'Oh, Daniel that's *great*,' Mandy said. 'A super pig.' Daniel added seven piglets and a blue and white striped milk jug. 'Bebby piglet food,' he said triumphantly.

Mandy and I decided, as we were burying the afterbirth, that we were certainly no loss to the teaching profession.

After Daniel went home there were a few weeks free until half term. In that time the two older sows, Phyll and Rosie, had litters of thirteen and fourteen, three more ducks hatched out clutches of eggs and the rabbits produced enough babies to populate Australia.

Parsley's puppies were soon racing round the house and garden and Ella became one of their gang. She towered over them but had no idea of her physical superiority and stayed about fourth in the pecking order. Their ringleader was Ellington (all the puppies had jazz names to match Ella) who got them into all sorts of scrapes from falling into the garden pond to gnawing at the bottom of the feed bags and releasing mountains of pig nuts all over the floor. Summer-born puppies seem more high spirited than those born in winter, or perhaps it's just that there is more day to be naughty in. At any rate they were too much of a handful to sleep in the kitchen at night, so we rigged up a night nursery out of straw bales in one of the stables.

Going out for early morning feeds in June was something I wouldn't have missed for a million pounds. The cobbled yard took on a pinkish hue as the sun came up and the low lying mist on the fields beyond the stables made a perfect foil for the lovely old stone walls. The scene cried out for an artist to come and capture it but the nearest we ever got was when Brian took a photograph of the manure heap which had reached a record temperature of 180°F and was steaming away like a train.

As soon as the puppies in the stables heard the clunk of the gate latch they started clamouring for food. The only way to stop the shrill seagull-like chorus was to put down bowls of milk and cereal. While they were eating, I fed the lambs, then the ducks and ducklings. Then I opened the stable doors and sat on the gate to watch them all troop out and greet each other.

Honda and Suzuki sprang round the yard like yoyos watched by the puppies whose stomachs were too full of breakfast to allow for early morning gymnastics. The ducklings waddled down their ramp one at a time and if their mothers weren't watching they would try and get pally with the puppies. Flicka was the only duck mother who allowed her children to mix with riff-raff, the others would quack with annoyance and tweak the puppies' tails with their beaks.

Once, for an experiment, I shut the senior ducks in and for ten blissful minutes I was able to watch the puppies and ducklings playing together. At no time did a puppy try to harm a duckling even when they shared the same food dish. It was a wonderful sight but I only did it once because the poor mother ducks became quite hysterical with anxiety.

All too soon the puppies were ready to be sold. I advertised them in a local paper: 'Carpets wrecked and furniture ruined in return for kind home and four meals a day', it said. Nobody could say we didn't comply with the Trades' Description Act.

The five puppies were all bought by 'real doggy people' as Mandy would say. One brought great luck to her new owners, a young couple who had been told they couldn't have children and had decided to settle for a dog instead. Within a few months of buying the puppy they found there was a baby on the way. Everyone knows that pets are supposed to be good for psychologically-disturbed people, but I have never heard of them being fertility charms too.

Ella's training began in earnest once the puppies had gone. Brian and I are normally pretty strict with puppies as we can't stand neurotic adult dogs but with Ella we found strictness wasn't necessary. She learned to walk to heel after one ten-minute lesson, and would sit on command and come when called without having to be taught. She didn't like riding in the car though, and we had to take her for short drives every day for a few weeks before she learned to sit quietly in the back. On one of these outings I saw a woman with a cavalier in her car and, forgetting it was Ella I had in the back, I wound down my window and called 'Snap!' She drove on with a bewildered expression on her face, probably wondering what sort of an idiot thought a cavalier looked like a collie.

Ella still played with Honda and Suzuki who, at ten weeks old, were getting quite rough, butting her with their hard heads. We had foolishly got too fond of them to be able to keep them for meat, so we swapped them (with a cash adjustment) for two three-day-old lambs, Ned and Nod. Ella did quite a double-take when she first saw Ned and Nod but she was soon licking them and teaching them how to chase her.

It seemed harmless enough fun at the time. It was only in later years, when we had a proper flock of sheep, that we regretted her earlier relationship with lambs. There she would stand, looking every inch the professional collie with her lovely coat and aristocratic face and on the command 'fetch' she would bound away from the flock and proudly *lead* them home. We always had to get our sheep dipped and wormed and sheared when nobody was watching unless we wanted to be the butt of local farmers' jokes.

Another stupid thing we did was to be too casual about the birth of Elizabeth's calf. We knew heifers must be watched closely when they calve, but instead of taking it in turns to sit with her round the clock when the calf was due, we checked at midnight that labour hadn't started, set the alarm for 5 a.m. and went to bed.

To our horror and everlasting shame Elizabeth's perfect little calf was born in the night and died because we were not there to break the birth sac. Elizabeth herself might have tried to do it, but the sac was an exceptionally tough one and being a heifer, she just hadn't the experience to cope.

We were fraught with guilt and depressed for ages afterwards. And to make matters worse, Elizabeth 'adopted' Brian – who was the first person to milk her after the birth – as her calf. She lavished all her maternal feelings on him, licking his face and following him around. It wasn't until she gave birth to her second calf the following year that she demoted Brian to grandson status. Perhaps we should have bought a calf or two for her to rear but we were in a frame of mind when we felt we were not fit to keep a goldfish let alone a cow.

Before long Elizabeth was giving five gallons of milk a day and with no guests in the house we could have bathed in it. Each lamb had two pints a day and the three dogs and two cats took care of a further two between them. The remainder was skimmed for the lactating sows and we made butter with the cream.

Home-made butter is strange stuff. It tastes of whatever the cow has been eating. If she ate watercress from the stream the following day's butter would be tangy and if she ate wild garlic it would be inedible. Butter from Jersey cows is so yellow it looks dyed and try as we might, we still preferred good old factory-produced Lurpak to our own wholesome produce.

We wanted everything to run extra smoothly when the next lot of guests came – the school party with its own staff. Mandy and I reorganised the two freezers and planned the meals. We frightened the lives out of ourselves when we came to write everything down. There would be twenty-six (counting the three of us) head of humans to feed three times a day for seven days. Admittedly the lunches would be packed ones but even 26 packed lunches take 104 slices of bread and 52 slices of something inside.

'Chicken,' said Mandy, scanning the list of things that were in the freezer. 'We're low on chicken.'

We looked at each other glumly. Outside in the poultry runs were twenty-four table birds which were now ready for killing. I had been hoping that some friendly out-of-work butcher would drop by one day in search of casual labour but he had not materialised.

'Let's do it ourselves,' said Mandy. 'When Brian goes to Taunton on Tuesday. You know how he hates killing them.'

'And we don't, I suppose? Have you ever killed a chicken?'

'No. You wring their necks, don't you?'

'Not personally I don't. I really couldn't do it like that. Brian says he's always scared he'll underkill them.'

We mulled over the problem for a day or two, and when Brian set out for Taunton on Tuesday morning were no nearer a solution. It was a kind thought of Mandy's to want to spare Brian the ordeal and it was certainly my turn to do a share of the dirty work.

'We could shoot them with an air gun,' Mandy suggested.

'Don't be daft Mandy, we'd probably miss or shoot each other or the cat. What else?'

'You've been on all these famous courses. How do they teach you to do it?'

'Wringing their necks, and that brings us back to square one. There's the broomstick method that they showed us for geese and turkeys but I've never done it.'

'Show me the broomstick method,' said Mandy. Just then the phone rang and I went to answer it. It was the mother of a booked-in child and I had to have quite a long conversation with her.

When I went back to Mandy I found her sitting on the wood pile with a headless cockerel in one hand and a lake of blood at her feet.

'I did one,' she said with a watery grin. 'I chopped his head off with the axe.'

'Strewth Mandy, what a lot of blood. Where's the head?'

'It went that-a-way.'

'It was jolly brave of you to do it on your own, only twenty-three to go, ha ha.'

'You do the next one.' She handed me the axe. 'I'll hold it and you chop.'

There are some things that get easier with practice. Chopping chickens' heads off is not one of them. There was no doubt it was quite the quickest and most humane way, but the *mess*. After we had done twelve, the chopping block was swimming in blood and we looked like characters in a Hammer film.

'Stop,' I said, retrieving head number twelve. 'We'll try the broomstick method.'

This was just as unpleasant but the area looked less like a haemophiliacs' convention afterwards and there were no severed heads to collect.

We started plucking and continued until our fingers were sore. After we had done four each we went indoors for elevenses and were still there half an hour later when Brian returned. He strode into the kitchen whistling cheerily as is his wont on a sunny June morning and stopped dead in his tracks when he caught sight of us.

'*Christ*!' he said, and reached for the teapot. 'What's happened?'

'We've got a surprise for you,' Mandy said, through a mask of blood and feathers.

'Mandy,' said Brian firmly. 'Whatever you've got for me couldn't possibly be a surprise. You've given me heart failure already. Now let me guess — a man-eating tiger in the sitting room? A rabid dog? Runaway steamroller?'

'We've killed all twenty-four chickens,' Mandy said proudly. 'Just the two of us.'

'They must have put up a hell of a fight.' Brian chuckled at his own wit, then he realised what Mandy had said. 'You *what*? Oh that's terrific, it really is. I've been putting it off for days.'

'That's why we did it. You can count it as a birthday present,' I said.

'Half a birthday present actually,' said Mandy. 'We could do with a hand plucking the rest.'

Brian's other birthday presents were tools, clothes and a piece of Stilton. Nice enough in their way, but not in the same league as twenty-four dead chickens.

Chapter Ten

THE COACH bringing the Catholic school party swished to a halt outside our gate. The driver leaned out and called to Brian: 'OK to park here, Squire? I don't think she'll go through the gateway.'

'That's fine where you are,' Brian said, and walked round to the side door to greet everyone.

'No nun?' whispered Mandy, as she caught sight of the three teachers.

'Ssh,' I said. I felt distinctly butterflyish about playing host to professionals. Two young teachers climbed down the coach steps and introduced themselves as Pam and Jane, then a sensible looking middle-aged woman in a cotton dress and cardigan got out.

'This is Sister Bridget,' said Pam.

'How do you do, Sister?' Brian said this in such a normal voice I couldn't look at Mandy in case we got the giggles. Brian had been practising his 'How do you do, Sister' for days, mainly in a Humphrey Bogart voice out of the side of his mouth.

By the time the three of us had 'how do you do'd' the three of them and they had said that they had had a pleasant journey (all lies of course, nobody has a pleasant journey with twenty children), the coach driver had unloaded the luggage on to the grass verge.

At a signal from Pam the children got down from the coach in twos and went over to the pile of suitcases where they stood quietly waiting for further instructions. Each child was then given its own case to carry and, still in twos, they formed a crocodile and walked down the drive. Nobody ran or shrieked or had to be told not to sniff and Brian asked Sister Bridget if they were sedated.

'They're too good to be true,' he said, and Sister laughed.

'Do you hear that, children?' she called. She had a lovely Irish brogue. 'Mr Addis was just saying what a grand bunch you are, isn't that a compliment now?' She turned back to Brian. 'They're overwhelmed,' she said. 'Most of them have not been out of London before. They've been talking of nothing else but this holiday for weeks. Oh!' She stopped suddenly as we turned the corner where the drive widened out and the view of the Otter valley made its greatest impact. 'What a beautiful view,' she said.

'Int there a lot of it, Miss?' observed one of the children to Jane, the youngest teacher. The crocodile broke ranks and an excited chattering broke out.

'That's the horizon over there.'

'Why aren't there no houses? Where does everyone live?'

'I can see a norse.'

'That's a cow, stupid. It's a cow, innit Miss?'

The three teachers ushered them into the house. We introduced them to the dogs and showed them to their bedrooms. While they unpacked, Mandy made a pot of tea for the teachers and some squash for the children. We could hear their shrill voices on the floor above: 'Cor, look at that ceiling, it's got great lumps of wood sticking out.'

'How about the garden then — it's bigger'n a cemetery.'

'There's some more view from my bedroom window — look Miss, there's a canal.'

'It's a river, Kevin,' one of the teachers said. 'The River Otter. Do you remember we looked it up on the map at school?'

'It's not like the Thames, is it, Miss?'

I showed Sister Bridget to her room. 'We've put you here in the chalet, Sister,' I said. 'There's a small double room next to yours which we've made up for two of the boys but the rest of the children are in the main house. We thought you'd get a bit more privacy here. The bathroom's in there, and if you want to use any of the empty rooms you're welcome.'

'It's truly lovely,' said Sister, gazing out of the huge south-facing window. The sun was obligingly setting in just the right place to cast a rosy glow over the panoramic view which was our greatest asset. 'You've gone to a lot of trouble to make us comfortable,' she said, looking approvingly round her bedroom which Mandy and I had gone to town on to make a good impression. 'And I'm sure we're going to love it here.'

'I do hope so. We've not had a school party before so please let us know if there's anything we've forgotten, won't you? What time would you like supper by the way?'

'Well, speaking for myself, I'm starving,' said Sister, dispelling yet another of my illusions about nuns. I imagined they were so busy thinking holy thoughts that they were above hunger. 'And I expect the others are too. We had lunch rather early on the coach.'

'Right, I'll get cracking then. Mandy will bang the gong in about half an hour.'

I shut myself in the kitchen and turfed the dogs and cats outside so that I could concentrate. Mandy and I had prepared the vegetables and fruit beforehand so there was no problem in that department. It was the fish that was bothering me. My ex-Catholic friend had been adamant about fish on Fridays and this was Friday.

When the potatoes had nearly boiled I put the vegetables on and cooked the fish carefully. There were thirty nice plump pieces of cod and these I egged and crumbed and lowered in to the deep fryer in batches of ten. I lit both ovens and put the plates and the cooked fish inside to keep hot. So far so good.

Mandy came in. 'How's it going?'

'Stupendously well. I can't understand it — nothing's gone wrong. Look at that fish.' I opened the oven door and showed Mandy twenty pieces of perfectly browned fish looking like a cookery book illustration.

'Only ten to do. Could you mash the potatoes please, Mandy, then go and bang the gong.'

While the children and teachers were settling themselves in the dining room, I strained the vegetables, finished the fish and laid out twenty-six hot plates on the kitchen tops. Mandy came in just as I had dished up and I handed her the first tray of plates to take through.

'Stop,' she whispered. 'We can't serve yet. They're going to say grace.'

'Oh hell, I forgot grace. I suppose you couldn't ask Sister to

95

make it snappy, could you? The food will get cold otherwise.'

'No, I jolly well couldn't. Anyway, she's started. Listen.' She opened the door a crack and we heard Sister Bridget saying, 'Bless us, O Lord, and the fruits of the earth and its waters here spread before us. Bless the friends who are here to share our holiday, the lovely beasts and beautiful birds and plants that enrich your world. May our days be filled with the warmth of your shining sun and all our activities find favour in your eyes. Amen.'

The children echoed 'amen' and everyone sat down. Mandy and I whizzed in with the rapidly cooling fruits of the earth and when the last person had been served they all set to.

I think Sister Bridget must have had a quiet word with her God about the food. The meal was such a resounding success even Brian blinked with amazement and asked if I had got outside caterers in.

After supper Mandy and I cleared the tables and Brian said he would feed the animals. 'Anyone like to help?' he asked, and twenty hands shot up.

'Me, Sir.'

'And me, Sir.'

'Can I put my wellingtons on? Mum said farmyards are ever so muddy.'

'Have you got a bull, Sir?'

'Can I feel a new laid egg?'

'Children, children,' said Sister Bridget quietly. 'Mr Addis doesn't want to hear such a racket. Now go and change into your wellingtons and we'll all go and see the animals.'

The children sped upstairs and Sister Bridget said to Brian: 'You must be very fond of children, Mr Addis.' Brian said it was not so much a love of children as fear of the bank manager, and Sister thought this was a great joke and said: 'Go on with you — you've got a heart of gold.'

'Flint would be nearer the mark,' I muttered to Mandy as we loaded the trolley. 'She should hear him doing his nut over hoof marks in the lawn.'

'Or puppies peeing on the carpet,' Mandy agreed. Brian overheard us but goldenheartedly decided not to start a debate about hoof marks and puppies.

Pam offered to give us a hand with the washing up. I started a half-hearted protest but Mandy had no such inhibitions and put a pile of clean drying up cloths on the table. 'You'll find the towelling ones are best,' she said.

'Mandy,' I said, but Pam laughed. 'No, really I'd like to help. Sister and Jane can easily manage without me and it's nice to have a break from the kids.'

'They're awfully well behaved, aren't they?' I said. 'Are they always so good?'

'Yes, on the whole it's a nice bunch – one of the best fourth years we've had. There's a boy called John who can get a bit bolshie as you'll probably find out before long. We've put him and his mate Terry in the chalet bedroom next to Sister so she can keep an eye on him.'

'Sister's great, isn't she?' said Mandy. 'Not a bit like you imagine a nun.'

'She's a dear,' Pam agreed. 'The children adore her. She never raises her voice at them you know. Jane and I bellow till we're blue sometimes, then Sister will come along and say 'children children' in that soft voice and get them eating out of her hand.'

'Do you take it in turns to go away on these field trips with them or do you volunteer?'

Pam laughed. 'We "volunteer" like you do in the army. Actually, we all wanted to come on this one because you're a small family concern. Sometimes there are other schools sharing the Centres and you can imagine the mayhem when you've got up to a hundred kids under the same roof.'

'And what's your programme for the week? I've had the rough draft from your school secretary, but there are five free periods in between your organised sight-seeing outings. Would you like me to get some leaflets from the library about local places of interest?'

Pam shuddered. 'No thanks. The set programme looks daunting enough. Have you ever taken a party of kids to a lace factory or a butterfly farm? No? Lucky you. What we'd really like to do, if you don't mind, is to stay here for the free periods. We'd keep the kids occupied so they wouldn't bother you.'

'That would be fine. There's seven acres for them to play in and you can use the playroom on wet days.'

'Thanks. Perhaps the kids will do their written work in there. They're keeping nature notebooks this week and they've got to write something every day about what they've been doing.'

'What do you do on Sundays?' Mandy asked. 'Do they go to church?'

'Yes. Sister Bridget will take them to church in the morning and the rest of the day is free.'

'Don't you and Jane go to church?'

'No, we're not Catholics. How about you?'

'We're atheists, I don't know about Mandy. What are you Mandy?'

'I'm a heathen according to my parents. Better not tell Sister B though or she might think it's her duty to try and save me.' We all giggled and the last sliver of ice was broken.

During the evening the children wrote letters home to let their parents know they had arrived safely. Once they were in bed, Pam and Jane brought the batch of letters into the sitting room, ostensibly to check that the envelopes were correctly addressed. The three teachers read through the letters and started smiling.

'Are you feeling strong?' Pam asked, and passed the letters across the table.

Seventeen out of the twenty children had drawn a picture of their dinner. The other three had launched straight into words: 'There was fish and raspberries and cream in a big jug and pink ice cream for people who do not like cream.' and 'The farmer is a kind old man and the farmer's wife cooks a lot of dinner.' Another had noticed that the pigs had spots but had forgotten to put the word 'pigs' so Sister corrected the sentence in case the child's mother thought there was a measles epidemic.

One bore no relation whatsoever to reality. It was a long letter, well composed and with no spelling errors. All it lacked was a vestige of truth. Who were these cider swigging yokels who had given the letter writer a ride on the creaking hay cart? And how had we overlooked the fine team of Suffolk Punches with their glittering horse brasses?

'That one's priceless,' I said, handing it to Brian who was still recovering from being called a kind old man.

'Oh, Frances.' The teachers laughed and Sister said: 'Whatever subject Frances starts on, she'll end up writing about horses. I thought I'd catch her out one day. I set them a composition where they had to describe an imaginary shipwreck. Well, you wouldn't think you could bring a horse into a shipwreck, would you? But Frances did. She turned herself into a mermaid, captured a sea horse and rode to safety.' She returned to the pile of letters. 'Listen to this one,' she said. 'The puppy is called Ella, she is lovely and infectionate.' Shall I correct "infectionate"?'

'I like infectionate,' said Brian. 'It's quite a good summing up of a dog, isn't it?'

'This one will confuse the parents,' Jane said: 'Freezing cows are black and white but our farmers got a jersey which is brown called Elizabeth. I must say I love "our" farmer, don't you?'

We all helped to seal and stamp the envelopes and Pam checked the addresses against her master list. 'There,' she said, 'that's day one finished.'

'It beats television any day, those letters,' said Mandy.

'Oh, you've seen nothing yet, Mandy dear,' said Sister. 'You wait until they hand in their nature notebooks for marking.'

'Where are you taking them tomorrow?'

'Fossil hunting at Lyme Regis in the morning, picnic lunch and then a free afternoon.'

The school's itinerary was arranged so that they had a coach outing every day. Some days they stayed out until suppertime but mainly the outings would only take a few hours and the rest of the time was free.

On their first free period the children waited in an agony of suspense while Mandy and I prepared the ponies for them to go riding.

'What's the big one's name, Miss?' asked John, the boy who was alleged to be bolshie.

'Monty,' said Mandy.

'I'll ride Monty then. My uncle's got a stud farm in Cork. I'm an expert rider.'

'Mind your manners, John dear,' Sister reproved. 'Mandy

will decide which pony is the most suitable.'

'I want the biggest,' John persisted. 'Where do you keep the whips, Miss?'

'No whips, John,' said Mandy. 'Ponies don't need whips.'

'How can you make them gallop then? Jockeys have got whips. Haven't jockeys got whips, Sister?'

'John,' said Sister firmly. 'Will you hold your tongue about whips. Now Mandy, which children would you like first, please?'

Mandy ran her eye over the children, assessing heights and weights. 'You, you, you and you,' she pointed, 'on Wellington, Rocky, Owen and Noah, in that order. And would you take Monty, Sister, please? You'll find him very quiet and comfortable.'

'Mercy me, he looks enormous. I haven't ridden in years,' said Sister. She mounted and adjusted the leathers proficiently. The children gaped in admiration and made remarks like, 'Fancy — Sister's on an 'orse' and 'She'll damage herself at her age'.

Mandy and I helped the children to mount. 'Would you like to lead off, Sister?' I said. 'We'll walk down to the river and then give the next lot a turn.'

The ponies ambled along in single file followed by Pam and Jane with the rest of the children. At first the riders squealed with excitement and fear, and clutched the fronts of the saddles with rigid fingers, but after a while they relaxed and copied Sister Bridget who was happily clopping along in front.

After half an hour they had had enough and willingly dismounted. They staggered around on bow legs, saying 'oo me bum' but recovered quickly enough to give the next lot of riders the benefit of their experience.

'Lean over when you go round corners.'

'Talk to him and he'll wiggle his ears.'

'Your wellies'll fall off if you don't keep your feet in the stirrups.'

Mandy said: 'Do you want to have a rest, Sister, or carry on on Monty? Or change to another pony if you like.'

'Monty and I are getting on splendidly,' said Sister. 'I'd like to carry on if it doesn't make things difficult for the children's turns.'

'No, that's OK. We can do them in fours until you're tired. Right, who's next?'

'Please take John,' said Pam. 'He's driving us potty with his boasting.'

Mandy whispered to me: 'I think we'll let Noah take care of young Willie Carson, don't you?' and I smiled to myself and nodded. We gave the next three children a leg up on to their ponies, then it was John's turn.

'Don't need a leg up on a titchy thing like that,' he said scornfully. 'I told you, I'm an expert.'

'Well, hurry up expert,' said Mandy. 'Show us how to do it.'

John seized Noah's saddle in both hands and tried to pull himself up with his arms. The saddle slid down Noah's ribs until it was nearly under his belly. The children nudged each other and giggled. 'Thought you was an expert, John,' someone called.

I replaced the saddle and tightened the girths.

'Put your left foot in the stirrup, John, and spring up off your right leg,' I said. John put so much effort into his spring that he vaulted clean over Noah's back and landed on the grass on the other side. The children collapsed with laughter and John got up, rather red in the face.

'It's because he's so *small*,' he explained. 'I'm used to riding racehorses.'

I gave him a leg up and we moved off. 'Giddy up,' John shouted, his confidence restored now that he was aloft. He held the reins like a charioteer and urged Noah to go faster by flapping them up and down. I had the other end of the reins in my hand so that Noah wouldn't get jabbed in the mouth. 'Why are you waving the reins about, John?' I said.

'I want to go faster, Miss.'

'You'll fall off if you go faster. You don't look too secure now and Noah's only walking.'

'Oh go on, Miss, be a sport. I want to gallop.'

'How about a little trot first?' I suggested, winking at Mandy. 'Then we'll see about a gallop. OK?'

'Trotting's kid's stuff. *Anyone* can trot. How do you get him going?'

'Just say "trot on" and when you want to stop say "whoah".

Ready?' I led Noah on to the soft grass and unclipped the leading rein.

'Trot on,' said John. Noah looked at me for confirmation as if to say 'Do you really know what you're doing?' before breaking into his brisk high-stepping trot.

'Whoah!' John yelled, as he felt himself sliding sideways. Noah stopped. Poor John.

He picked himself up from the ground for the second time.

'How about a gallop now, John?' Mandy said, keeping a straight face.

'Or having a ride on Monty?' I added.

'No fear.' John accepted a helping hand and remounted. 'It's bad enough falling off a little 'un — I'd break me neck if I fell off Monty.'

He was a brave and cheerful boy and for all his boasting there was something very endearing about him. I think the uncle's stud farm was about as real as Frances's mermaid, at any rate he didn't mention it at all after his tumbles.

Sister Bridget had a wonderful knack of nipping trouble in the bud. At the first hint of bad language or quarrelling she would say, 'You seem to have plenty of spare energy Terence', (or Maureen or, more usually, John). Let's see what little chores we can find to do, shall we?' and the child in question would be set a small boring task like clearing the tables or tidying the playroom. One day this technique backfired.

Terence, or Terry as we called him, had misbehaved at the beach and had refused to apologise to a buxom lady holiday-maker after he had called her ten-ton tits. On their return Sister asked us if there were any chores we would like done as Terence was on the mat.

'He could clean some of the bridles,' Mandy suggested. 'They haven't been done for ages.' She took Terry to the tack room and showed him how to use saddle-soap and water to remove the sweat stains on the leather. Terry settled himself on an upturned bucket and got to work.

'It's not *fair*.' Frances, who spent all her spare time getting drunk on the leathery smell in the tack room, wanted to clean bridles too.

'OK. OK. Keep your hair on,' Mandy said. 'You can clean the saddles if you like. Get a sponge and a bucket and I'll show you how.'

Before long the bush telegraph was at work and all the children appeared in the stableyard begging to be allowed to work. Mandy fetched metal polish and had them all busily shining up the stirrups and bits. Sister Bridget roared with laughter when Mandy told her how popular Terry's 'punishment' was.

Weeding was another popular chore with the city children. They had to be closely supervised to make sure they didn't throw out the baby with the bath water, but on the whole their help was useful. One day, after a gardening session, some of the girls slipped back to the pansy bed and picked posies as a surprise for us.

'Thank you, dears,' Brian said through gritted teeth, 'but don't pick any more, will you? I'm growing them specially for seed. They have to bloom and die out of doors so that they make seeds.'

'Seems a waste,' said one of the girls. 'They're ever so pretty, aren't they? And there's hundreds left.' Brian groaned to himself.

'The farmer is a kind old man,' I reminded him after the girls had gone away.

'He won't be for much longer,' said Brian. 'The trouble is they're such *nice* kids – I can't possibly tell them off for picking a few flowers. But what with the cold start the pansies had this year, and losses through weeding, I really don't want any heads picked at all.'

'Never mind. The sweetpeas will be ready soon. It looks like being a bumper crop and we can let the kids pick any number. And talking of peas, do you know most of those kids didn't know how to shell peas? They'd never seen fresh ones before.'

Pea shelling had been duly recorded in the children's nature notebooks as 'one of the interesting things we did today'. The notebooks were a never ending source of interest to us. The teachers would bring them into the sitting room for marking after the children were in bed. What I found fascinating was their attention to minutiae – the ant on a leaf, the thinned out carrot too small to be eaten, the fact that piglets have eyelashes and so forth. You felt that if a herd of bison had appeared on the horizon it would have taken second place to the discovery of a maggot in a pea pod.

The teachers worked hard with the children, encouraging them to write about all their new experiences and to draw pictures when they found it too hard to express themselves in words.

'You're going for a walk this evening,' Pam told them after supper one day. 'In the country there are certain animals and birds that only come out at night. Can anyone tell me what we call creatures who wake up at night?'

Nobody could. 'They're called nocturnal creatures,' Pam continued undaunted. 'And can anyone tell me what particular animals or birds are nocturnal?' Three hands went up.

'Foxes, Miss?'

'And hedgehogs, Miss. They come out and get run over at night.'

'Our cat got run over,' contributed a small girl with braces on her teeth. 'Me dad dug a hole in the back garden, it was ever so sad.' Pam moved in swiftly before the owner of the late cat could get launched on a detailed chronicle.

'What other things might we see at night?' she persevered.

'Owls, Miss, and moles.'

'Not moles, Frances. Moles don't come out of their tunnels very often. But owls, yes, that's very good. Anything else? No? Well, I'll give you a clue. It doesn't have to be a bird or an animal.' The children scowled with concentration.

'A night watchman, Miss?' suggested John. Pam sighed and said: 'What about moths? You've all seen moths flying against the windows here, haven't you?' The children agreed that they had and wasn't it a lark trying to shoo them out of the bedrooms?

'And badgers,' concluded Pam. 'Badgers are very shy animals so when we go out for our walk tonight we'll try to be really quiet, then we might see one.'

This didn't meet with overwhelming enthusiasm and Sister Bridget chuckled and murmured quietly, 'If I was a betting woman I'd lay 100 to 1 against *that* particular possibility.'

As soon as dusk fell the school party set out, returning a

couple of hours later rather chilly and in need of hot cocoa.

Next day the notebooks recorded that the night smells stronger than the day and that Michael Murphy got a splinter in his thumb and was given a plaster. Nobody had seen any nocturnal creatures so they drew pictures of their own plim-solled feet walking along the black tarmac road. One child claimed to have seen a tiger and another wrote that he was frightened when Dick Turpin 'rained' in Black Bess on the road to Taunton. It went on: 'He told Sister Bridget he would clout her with his cutlass unless she paid him ransom. Sister said don't be silly Dick dear you know I have got no money and brave Dick Turpin gallupt in to the distance. Then we came home and had some cocoa.'

Pam gave this four out of ten for content and a gold star for neat handwriting.

Chapter Eleven

FOR THE REST of the summer season we took on three more assistants, Julian and Anne, who were both undergraduates, and Mary, a qualified teacher.

The first thing they wanted to know after they had unpacked and come downstairs for a cup of coffee was why we needed six staff for twenty children.

'Six isn't too many really,' Mandy said. She was a little defensive with the newcomers at first as up until then she had been 'head girl'. 'Brian and Faith have *got* to have some time off this year,' she went on. 'They knocked themselves out last year being with the kids seven days a week so it's up to us to see that they don't overdo things again.'

Brian, who was rather touched by Mandy's concern for our welfare, explained the set-up. 'Most of the children are very young – we take them from five you know – and it's a big adventure for them just being away from home. There has to be an adult on hand wherever they go, except the playroom – they can't really come to much harm in the playroom.'

Can't they, I thought, remembering how often the TV broke down last year, and how many times Brian had had to replace window glass after indoor shuttlecock tournaments.

'And the thing is they don't stay together in a group,' I said. 'At any given time there'll be some in the tree house, some playing in the hay, some watching the animals and some in the house. It'll be your job to keep an eye on every single one of them. I don't mean you have to breathe down their necks the whole time but you *must* know where they are and what they're doing.'

'What about outings?' Anne asked. 'How many do you take at a time?'

'All of them. We choose days when all of you are on duty –

you get a day off a week by the way — and we shoehorn them into the Transit and take them to the beach or to fêtes and things.'

'It's hell,' Mandy put in.

'*Mandy*, it's not that bad,' I protested.

'I agree with Mandy,' said Brian. 'They're fine for the first five minutes, then they start saying "Are we nearly there yet" and "What does congealed entrance mean" and then some will be sick and the rest will sing "Ten Green Bottles". I think hell is a fair description.'

Julian and Anne laughed at what they thought was an exaggeration, but Mary, who had done a year with a reception class nodded and said, 'What about shoes? I bet they lose their shoes all the time.'

'Shoes, towels, pocket money — you name it, they'll lose it,' said Mandy. 'One little cretin even lost his jeans at Lyme Regis. We spent hours combing the beach then he remembered he hadn't been wearing them after all. I could have strangled him.'

'We try not to strangle them though,' said Brian. 'The parents don't like it.'

'I'm against corporal punishment,' Julian said.

'So are we in principle,' said Brian, 'and in fact ninety-nine per cent of them are nice, uncomplicated kids, but you do get the odd one who'll try and chuck stones at the chickens or kick sand at people on the beach. You'll have to play it by ear if that happens — try a quick clout first and if that doesn't work send them to their room for an hour or so. Anyway, to get back to shoes. There's a big box just inside the utility room door. When you find shoes, socks, jumpers and so on, chuck them in the box and each evening we'll try and match them with their owners. Everything is supposed to be marked before they come, but a lot of it isn't or it's got smudged initials, and with most of the kids wearing identical Marks and Spencer gear it's virtually impossible to sort out.'

Mandy said she solved the problem like Robin Hood — 'You know, give out the bits and pieces to whoever seems to need it.' Mandy was nothing if not practical.

We showed Mary, Julian and Anne the wall chart on which

we had written down all the local events for the year. Agricultural shows, village fêtes and gymkhanas were the main attractions with occasional entertainments like the Honiton Traction Engine rally or the West Country Stallion parade.

'Do you ever take them to the cinema?' Mary asked.

'No, it's never crossed our minds. Last year we didn't have a single rainy day so there wasn't any need to think up wet day activities. It might be a good idea though, to get a programme from the cinema in Taunton in case we run out of ideas for rainy days. Can we leave that to you, workforce?'

'Workforce?' Julian and the others looked at each other and grinned.

'Well, staff then. I don't know what to call you. You're a cross between nannies, bodyguards and play-leaders.'

'We're minders,' said Mandy. 'Minders or downtrodden serfs.'

Next day the downtrodden serfs went to Taunton in Anne's car to do some research. They discovered a large Sports Centre in the nearby town of Wellington where admission charges were reduced for parties of ten or more, and three cinemas with programmes suitable for under-twelves.

Julian, who was a bit of a fitness enthusiast, gave me a list of equipment he thought would come in useful for organised sports competitions at home. I went to the Cash and Carry and piled the van up with twenty-four footballs, rope, white tape, prizes and coloured plastic buckets.

'Where are you planning to hold these sports, Julian?' I said, when we were unloading the van.

'In the top field. I thought we could shut the ponies and Elizabeth in the yard for a couple of hours, and rig up a track for games like egg and spoon and obstacle races. Oh good, you've bought plenty of bowls and buckets. I'll think up some water competitions for them.'

Meanwhile, as countdown approached, Sara, whom we had thought safely settled in London, wrote us a letter. She timed its arrival nicely — there was only one more day left before the first twenty summer holiday children came.

At the end of the first page, after a long preamble about mutual friends and the weather, she mustered enough courage to come to the point: 'I have met this super chap called Gerry,' she wrote, 'he is 6′1″, fair curly hair and blue eyes. I think you will like him, his main hobby is fly fishing. Anyway, we had this super idea – we have decided to have a –'

Feverishly flinging page one aside, I picked up the next page: '74 bus (the one that goes down Baker St) didn't come for over half an hour,' it said.

'Where the hell's page two, Brian?'

'You've got page two. I've got three and four. Bit complicated, isn't it?'

'*Complicated*? She's about to give birth to a 74 bus according to this. Here, let's have a look at your page three.'

Sara had misnumbered the pages. Three followed one so that it now read 'have decided to have a try at a caretaking job together. We have been for an interview and have been shortlisted. I thought it would be better to tell you in a letter because you will only start shouting if I phone.'

The letter went on to justify her decision to give up further education and to describe the job that she and her 6′1″ fisherman were hoping to get. 'And I hope you won't be too cross,' it concluded, 'but I had to lie about my age. They only want people over 21. Gerry is already quite old so he didn't have to lie.'

There was a P.S. 'Marcus helped an electrician friend to wire up Hornsey Town Hall for a special function. He *says* there is no connection with this cutting.' The enclosed newspaper cutting had a big black headline: CROUCH END IN MYSTERY BLACKOUT.

That at least made us laugh. Turn Marcus loose with a screwdriver and he could short circuit a torch, let alone a town hall.

'I don't like the sound of "Gerry is already quite old",' I said. 'How old is quite old?'

'When you're seventeen I suppose twenty-one seems quite old,' Brian said. 'I wonder how long she's known him.'

'I'll phone Marcus tonight and get the gory details. I do hope he's not forty or anything awful. I couldn't stand a son-in-law of forty.'

'She's not *marrying* him,' Brian pointed out. 'She's going caretaking with him.'

'I don't like the sound of that either.' Sara had said in her letter that her prospective employers had a small country estate which they only used at weekends, and that when the place was empty they used Securicor to patrol the grounds. 'If they've got valuables in the house, I shouldn't have thought a couple of youngsters would deter burglars.'

Soon we were so snowed under with holiday guests that there was no time to worry about Sara. She stayed well out of phone reach for a few days and all we could get out of Marcus was that Gerry was twenty-four and quite a nice bloke.

Nineteen children arrived on Saturday (the twentieth was coming later in the week) and we were back with endless cups of tea and conducted tours of the farm.

It was my bad luck to get lumbered with a dreadful little man, a caricature of an English colonial, who had the most outrageous ideas about child care. He wanted Jake — that was his six-year-old son — to be 'made a man of' and to this end he had encased the child in an outfit bristling with weaponry. There were toy hand grenades in the battledress pockets, a sheath knife, scout knife, two pistols and a cartridge belt. Poor Jake could hardly move with this lot dangling from D rings set into the pockets. The khaki denim suit was quite cute with its epaulettes and metal studs, but Jake looked so ill at ease in it I guessed it had not been his choice.

'Shall I show you to your bedroom, Jake?' I said. Jake was about to take my outstretched hand when his father snapped: 'Don't mollycoddle him.'

'Why not?' I said. 'It's the first time he's been away from home. He's probably a bit frightened.'

'Frightened? Damn it, he'd better not be. He's got to go to boarding school when he's seven. Don't suppose they'll hold his hand there, eh?'

'This isn't a school, and we shall treat Jake as we would our own son. Is your wife with you? I'd like to have a word with her.'

'No, she couldn't come. We had tropical disease jabs recently — we're going to Africa for our own holiday — and she's gone down with some 'flu thing. Caroline's around somewhere though, one of your girls is showing her the ropes.'

Caroline was Jake's seven-year-old sister and as she wasn't going to be made a man of she was happy as a lark. We ran her to earth halfway up the hollow oak tree, dangling upside down by her knees with Mandy ready to field her underneath.

'Little monkey,' said her father, permitting himself the luxury of a smile.

'Daddy, can you see me? Look, I'm up here.'

'Not much tearfulness there, eh?' said the father smugly.

'Your father's leaving now, Caroline,' I said hopefully. 'Are you coming down to say goodbye?' Caroline scrambled down the tree and hugged her father.

'Goodbye Daddy, bring us back something nice from Africa, won't you?'

'Goodbye poppet.' He kissed Caroline and shook hands with Jake. 'Chin up, old man. I expect the other boys will be green with envy when you show them your cap pistols, eh?'

'*Cap pistols*,' Mandy started. I gave her a warning look and she bit back whatever she was going to say about cap guns and animals.

We waved the father's car goodbye and the children ran back to the climbing tree. When they were out of earshot Mandy said: 'What a *horrible* man. I can just picture him in Africa, can't you? Giving the natives a touch of the bull whip to "teach them a lesson".'

'Or to make men of them,' I agreed. 'And bringing back their shrunken heads as souvenirs for the kids.'

'That boy's awfully stiff, isn't he? What's his name?'

'Jake. You'd be stiff in all that clobber. Could you disarm him please? I've got more parents to see. Be tactful, won't you?'

'Am I ever not tactful?' Mandy grinned. 'Hoy Tosh and you Caroline. Come down here a minute. I'll show you some baby ducklings.'

I saw to some more parents, then Brian presented me with a small boy called Adrian who had wet himself. This was nothing unusual for newcomers and in our experience it was only the boys who did it. I popped Adrian into the bath with some wooden sailing boats and while he was sinking the Bismarck I went to his room to fetch some dry clothes.

Returning to the bathroom I found Jake outside the door crying his eyes out, and Mandy trying to comfort him. 'He wet himself when he saw the ducklings splashing in their water bowl,' she said, and handed him over thankfully.

'Thanks, Mandy. I'll put him in with Adrian. Come on, Jake, let's make you a bit more comfortable.' Adrian peered over the rim of the bath.

'This is Jake, Adrian. Move over.'

'Hi, Jake,' said Adrian. 'You wet your pants too?'

'No, I *didn't*,' said Jake, crimson with embarrassment. 'The duck's water went all down me.' He started to cry again. 'You won't tell my daddy, will you?'

I stripped his clothes off, not without difficulty. There were so many studs and buckles it was like unharnessing a horse.

'I'm always doing it,' said Adrian cheerfully. He was a fat amiable boy who had arrived quite early in the day with his parents, two aunts and a spaniel. The whole family were fatties, even the dog, and everything they said was accompanied with great gales of laughter and wobbling chins. 'Me mum says I drink a lot and wee a lot. I 'spect you're the same. You coming in? The water's nice and hot.'

I lifted Jake into the bath and added some Matey to make froth. 'Play with the boats you two and I'll go and find some pants for Jake.'

When I got back Adrian was saying: 'Got a big winkle for six, haven't you? I'm nearly seven and mine's not nearly as big as yours.' Since Adrian was obviously heading straight for a first-class honours degree in applied psychology I withdrew and left him to continue the good work.

'Where are your clothes, Jake?' Caroline said later when Jake reappeared in soft cotton shorts and a T-shirt filched from the lost-property box.

'In the wash,' I said.

'What, all of them? He's got lots of new clothes in his case. Didn't you look in his case?'

I thought I had better come clean with this intelligent, lynx-eyed sister of his, so I said, 'All Jake's clothes are new, aren't they, Caroline?'

'Yes, mine too. We had a lovely day out buying things for

this holiday. We had lunch at Harrods, didn't we, Jake? It was yummy, we had chips and milk shakes.'

'New clothes,' I cut in, 'have some stiff stuff in the material. It's called "dressing".'

'Like dressing-gowns?'

'No, not like dressing-gowns. Anyway, it's very uncomfortable to wear stiff clothes and Jake had red marks on him where the material had rubbed. I expect your mummy forgot to soak the dressing stuff out before she packed.'

'Daddy did the packing actually. Mummy was ill after her vaccination. Are you going to unstiff Jake's shirts?'

'That's right. And his jeans. Meanwhile he can borrow some spare clothes.'

'I like these better,' said the ego-restored Jake. 'It says Arsenal FC on my front. What does it mean?'

'It's a football club in London. Doesn't your daddy take you to football matches?'

'No, he says football's rot. I've been to Lords though.'

The T-shirt jogged my memory: 'Where are your guns, Jake?'

'Mandy put them away. She said I'd better not have any of my guns and things because it might frighten the baby animals.'

'He never plays with them anyway,' said Caroline. 'He leaves them in his room when Daddy's at work.' For a minute they both looked a bit glum but soon brightened up when they heard promising sounds of a row brewing outside. It was Julian trying to reason with a small someone.

'You mustn't eat it,' Julian was saying. 'You don't know where it's been.'

'Yes, I do. I found it in the tree house.'

'But it's *solid*. It could have been there for weeks.'

'Go on, Julian. Be a sport. I'm starving.'

'No. Anyway, supper's nearly ready.' It was only after he had promised to explain how scientists carbon-date specimens that Julian was able to confiscate the wrinkled doughnut and escape.

At supper Julian and Anne already had the glazed look that you get when you've been trying to hold several conversations

113

at once at junior level. Mary, being a trained teacher was fine and told them a few trade secrets. Brian and I were pleased with our new team of minders, particularly when they pulled off the minor miracle of getting all the children in bed and asleep by 8 p.m. This meant that we could both go to that evening's SHA lecture (Comparative Manurial Values) instead of tossing for it.

The relative mineral composition of pigeon manures to pure (i.e. not mixed with straw) cow dung proved to be a study which, while not spellbinding, demanded concentration. It released us temporarily from thoughts of lost wellingtons and runny noses and, though we didn't know it then, was a small factor in deciding our farming future.

In common with our fellow smallholders we were 'land hungry'. It's an incurable disease of all small farmers and even the thirty-acre 'giants' in our group wouldn't be satisfied until they had fifty. We had seven acres – about average in the SHA – and a hefty overdraft. We dreamed of all the exciting things we could do with fifteen.

On Monday, Mandy and I drove to Exeter to collect the twentieth child, an eight-year-old called Toby who was coming by plane from the Channel Islands.

'I hope he's nice,' Mandy said. 'The other kids are getting on so well together he may find it difficult to fit in, coming two days late.'

'I bet you five bob he'll be the best of this week's kids,' I said.

'How much is five bob?'

'Sorry, twenty-five pence.'

'What makes you so sure he'll be nice?'

'Because his name's Toby. Don't ask me why but all Tobys and Ruperts are really nice kids and they've got super parents too.'

'Oh, go on. You can't go by names. Look at Jake, that's a nice name but his father's gruesome.'

'I didn't say *all* names, just Toby and Rupert. It's just one of those odd things I've noticed. I've never come across a nasty Toby or Rupert.'

'What about girls?'

'Well, all Mandys are big-headed twits. . .' I began.

We parked outside the airport building and walked across to the plate-glass doors of the reception area. It was a hot day and we were both wearing cut-down jeans, sleeveless cotton tops and espadrilles. I mention this because, in the light of what followed, we could only assume it was our scruffy appearance that caused the trouble.

Business was evidently not very brisk for the airport was more like a sleepy country railway station with only one man in charge. He was a vicious looking thug of about sixty, with close-cropped hair and a very thin-lipped face. He watched us walk towards the glass doors. We felt rather uncomfortable being stared at and Mandy started to clown at her reflection in the glass.

'Good afternoon,' I said. 'Lovely day, isn't it?'

'What's your business here?' said Hitler. Mandy, who afterwards admitted that the bad vibes he was giving off gave her the creeps, said cheerfully: 'Oh, we're going to plant a few bombs, hijack one or two planes – you know, the usual things.'

I have never seen Mandy come so near to being crushed by a look, but she nearly was then. Hitler poked his bristly face right up to her and said quietly: 'Don't get funny with me, Girlie. What do you want?'

'We've come to meet an unaccompanied boy on the Jersey plane,' I said, opening my bag and handing him Toby's name and flight number. He was disappointed that we had a right to be on his territory and stood aside to let us into the building. It was nice and cool in there and we flopped into chairs.

'God, what a creep,' said Mandy. 'I wonder what his job is. Do they have commissionaires at airports?'

'I don't know. Perhaps he's a public relations officer.' We looked round the deserted reception area and started laughing.

'Ssh, he's coming over.'

He looked bigger and more menacing indoors. He went over to a door marked 'Customs' and said: 'Come with me.' Mandy and I got up and tried to go through the doorway but he barred the way with crossed arms. 'Not you,' he said to Mandy, 'just your mother.'

'Why?' I said. 'We're together.' He ignored this and pointed to my shoulder bag: 'Leave that with the girl and follow me,' he said.

If the area had not then started filling up with people I would have thought we were having a bad dream. 'You can't be serious?' I said. I looked at the newcomers for support but they appeared to be kitchen staff, intent on their own jobs.

'No handbags in Customs,' said Hitler. He didn't actually say 'rules is rules' but it was written all over him.

'Oh, you're a *customs* officer,' Mandy said, as if that could explain his boorishness.

'Are you going to argue all day?' His neck was starting to go red.

'Give me your bag if it'll shut him up,' said Mandy, giving a surreptitious thumbs up. I got the message. 'Thanks Mandy, you can smuggle the state secrets and blackmail notes through, can't you?'

'Of course. No trouble. What about the microdot message on the Elastoplast?'

We kept this up until Hitler had shut the door between us. To my amazement he locked it and pocketed the key.

'You still there, Mandy? He's locked me in.'

'Yes, I'm here. Has he pulled your fingernails out yet?'

'Yes. And teeth.'

'I'll tell Brian you died bravely. What's it like in there?'

'It's a bit bleak. There's an advert for rabies and a set of parallel bars and a table. Nothing else.'

'You could do press-ups on the parallel bars.'

'Rather difficult with no fingernails.' Just then the Jersey plane landed and Hitler unlocked another door and went out. I started swinging on the parallel bars and was getting on nicely with half-remembered exercises when I became aware of a small boy watching me.

'Excuse me,' he said. 'I think they want to use the rails for us to check out.' I jumped down.

'Are you Toby?'

'Yes. Are you Mrs Addis?' I nodded and Toby said: 'I thought you'd be older.' He wore glasses.

Hitler re-entered and marshalled the Jersey passengers into a line. Each person had to walk between the parallel bars which were placed against the table, and wait while Hitler stared them out and chalked a mark on their luggage. He had the same unnerving effect on the incoming holiday makers as he had on us and I heard one of them say to her friend: 'If they're all like that in Devon, I'm going home.'

The relief of getting back to the car park in one piece sent us into fits of laughter. Toby, whose glasses gave him a misleadingly serious air, wanted to know what the joke was so we told him. He thought it funny to, but what really creased him was the sight of our car, the one that we had bought for £35 when the Transit was having a service.

'Does it actually go?' he wanted to know.

'Of course it goes,' Mandy said. 'Well, most of the time.'

'It's incredible,' he said, running his hand over the craters in the bodywork. 'It should be in a museum. Fancy it being roadworthy.'

'It's got six months MOT still,' I said. 'Top speed of thirty with a following wind. It's very heavy on water though.'

'Water? You run it on water?'

'And some petrol if it's good.' Mandy lifted the water drum off the back seat and filled the radiator. Toby thought the way the water ran out almost as fast as it went in, highly entertaining, and begged to be allowed to do the next three re-fuellings on the way home.

He phoned his mother as soon as we got back. 'Mummy, I'm going to love it here,' he said. 'They've got an old banger like something out of Beaulieu and Mandy does *brilliant* Gestapo voices.' I grabbed the phone before he could ring off. The poor woman needed some reassuring that her son had come to the right place.

Chapter Twelve

WHEN ONE OF THE broody bantams was savaged by a cat one day, nobody thought it could survive. We opened the stable where several ducks, chickens and bantams were sitting on their respective clutches of eggs, and were horrified to see a bloody heap of feathers lying on the ground by the nesting boxes.

The heap turned out to be a bantam, still breathing but with blood seeping out of a wound in her throat. Her neck appeared to be broken.

I ran indoors and fetched a tea tray to use as a stretcher. It was 6 a.m. and nobody had surfaced yet so we decided to examine her on the kitchen table. Easing her carefully on to the tray so as not to cause any more injuries, Brian carried her while I gathered up the still warm eggs in the nesting box.

'What are you going to do with the eggs?'

'I'll put them in the linen cupboard. They're due to hatch any time now and I don't think we've got another broody to finish incubating them. I'll have to hatch them out on a hot-water bottle.'

The bantam kept opening and shutting her beak as though gasping for air. Brian watched her for a few moments while I got the animal first-aid box. 'I think it would be kinder to kill her,' he said. 'She's lost a lot of blood.'

'Give me ten minutes to have a look,' I said. 'See her eyes? They're not cloudy yet. I don't think she's given up.'

'I'll go and start the feeds then. Give me a shout if you want me to kill her.'

I swabbed away the trickling blood and clipped off all the feathers round the injured neck. The torn skin revealed a massive flesh wound but there was no arterial bleeding.

'Hells bells,' said Mandy, appearing at my elbow suddenly. 'What's happened?'

'Cat, I should think. Do you think potassium permanganate would be safe for a wound this size?' Mandy tied a clean tea towel over her mouth to prevent human germs making things worse, and examined the bleeding area closely. 'I should think so,' she said. 'The artery's OK. But you'd better hurry up before she snuffs it.'

'Crush an arnica tablet for me in a teaspoon, would you. We'll mix it with water and trickle it down her throat.' While Mandy was doing this I covered the bleeding wound with potassium permanganate crystals. The bleeding stopped immediately and we sighed with relief. We washed our hands and the torn pieces of the bantam's skin in Dettol, and gently replaced the skin over the flesh, rearranging the jagged edges like the pieces of a jigsaw puzzle. We were suffocating inside our tea-towel masks and Mandy said she wished she'd stayed in bed. 'Cosmetic surgery's not my scene really, not before breakfast.'

'Stop moaning. How many National Hunt jockeys can say they've been on the *active* side of an operation? Is that arnica ready?'

The arnica was a homeopathic preparation, sometimes very effective for shock. We filled a dropper and I held the bantam's beak open with tweezers while Mandy slowly dripped the fluid down its throat. Not much was wasted and the bird stopped the distressing 'gaping' action.

We put her on a towel-wrapped hot-water bottle in a cardboard box and left her in the sitting room, the only quiet spot in the house. Every hour I woke her up, turned her on to her other side and repeated the arnica dose. By lunchtime she was no better so I started two-hourly doses of glucose as well.

It seemed hopeless. There she lay, on the brink of death, almost comatose. The neck would begin to scab over quite healthily and a few phone calls to SHA members who were experienced with poultry confirmed my opinion that a dressing wasn't necessary. 'She'll die though,' they all said knowingly, 'she'll have no reserves if she's been sitting on eggs. You know how thin they get when they're broody — that's all they live for, the eggs.'

Next morning, surprised to find her still alive, I gave her a liquid feed with the dropper — glucose and multivitamins added – and carried her out to the farmyard. She lay in her box quite inert while I clanked and banged and clucked to the other birds as I fed them. The cockerel crowed. Surely *that* will ring a bell, I thought, but she made no response. She wasn't asleep though, her eyes were wide open and she stared apathetically into space.

I covered the box with wire netting to stop the chickens pecking at her scabs – chickens have no finer feelings towards their injured mates – and went indoors to start the breakfasts. There was a lot of oohing and aahing coming from upstairs which I thought meant the dogs were in the bedrooms again. Then Mandy came down, carrying a seed tray full of newly hatched chicks.

'Seven out of seven,' she said. 'We heard them cheeping in the airing cupboard.' The children begged to be allowed to touch them and sat cross-legged on the floor in various stages of undress while we let them hold a chick in turn.

'Aren't they darlings? So *tiny*.'

'Why are they black? I thought chicks were yellow.'

'Can we give them toast for breakfast? Or do they eat eggs? We saw eggshells in the airing cupboard.'

Mandy explained that newborn chicks don't eat for some hours after they're hatched. 'They've got to have a sleep first,' she said. 'They get very tired pecking their way out of the eggs, so they have to rest before they can eat.'

'And while they're resting, you can have your breakfast,' I said. 'Go and get dressed, you can see them again later on.'

Anne and Julian took over the cooking, Mandy went upstairs to do shoelaces, and I carried the chicks out to the yard where we had prepared a mesh coop for them.

The bantam was just as I'd left her, lying on her side, breathing quietly. 'That's all they live for, the eggs.' The sentence floated into my mind. On impulse I tipped the seven chicks into her box: 'Say hullo to your mum, kids.'

And then there was the nearest thing to a miracle that I'm ever likely to see. The high-pitched cheeping of her seven babies cleaved through the fogged brain of the invalid and galvanised her into action. She gave a few strangled clucks and struggled to roll on to her front. She was terribly weak and I had to help her into a squatting position. Her eyes brightened and focused on the chicks, then she spread her wings out and shook her feathers. She held her head sideways — it was obviously very stiff and reminded me of Marcus in his surgical collar — but everything seemed to be intact. She could see, hear and feel the chicks and with a bit of luck, once her throat was less sore, would be able to talk to them.

The chicks burrowed under their mother's wings and I left the little family mutually supporting each other for a couple of hours. After that she never looked back. She had to be hand fed for a week as her neck was too stiff for her to reach down and peck, but the wound didn't go septic.

The idea that seven demanding infants could be instrumental in rescuing someone with one foot in the grave seemed inconceivable to Julian and Anne when, a few days later, the four minders took all twenty children to the cinema. Mandy and Mary hadn't any illusions to start with so the ordeal came as no surprise to them.

The party returned home, the children full of pent-up energy and Julian and Anne still shell-shocked.

'Sit down, have a cup of tea, and tell us what happened,' Brian said, shooing ten spacemen out of the kitchen so that we could hear ourselves speak.

It was a wet day in the middle of the school holidays, so the cinema had been packed. There were not enough empty seats for all twenty-four to sit together and they split up. Julian and Anne sat at each end of a row with twelve kids between them. Mandy and Mary took four each and sat in different rows some way back.

The lights went down and the film started. One of our boys, struggling to find his place in the dark pushed a cornet of soft ice cream into a man's face. The man got angry and the boy cried because he had wasted his ice cream. Julian went to buy him another to shut him up.

Meanwhile at Anne's end of the row, a seven-year-old girl decided to share her popcorn with her sister. This would have been all right if her sister hadn't been sitting in Mary's group five rows back. Her aim backfired and the bag of popcorn sailed across the heads of the audience, scattering its sticky contents on the way.

Julian returned to his seat and handed the new ice-cream cornet to the child next to him to pass along the row to the boy who had lost his. By the time it reached its destination it had been sampled by eight tongues and was a shadow of its former self. This led to a punch-up and two adults who were sandwiched in between the children got up and left to find better seats. The popcorn-sharing girl called to her sister that there were now two spare seats.

While everybody moved up one to enable the sisters to sit next to each other, Anne had to whisk another child, whose lunch was threatening to reappear, to the Ladies. When they returned their seats had been taken by two from Mary's group, so they went and sat with Mary. This left Julian in sole charge of fourteen. He gave up the unequal struggle and turned a deaf ear to the consumption of fourteen cans of 7 Up and the chorus of burps which immediately followed.

During the interval the children re-armed with sweets, nuts, popcorn and drinks. They all promised to be good for the remainder of the programme.

Being 'good' evidently didn't mean being quiet. The terrible twenty, seated together for the second half as other members of the audience had moved out of range, chatted non stop. They compared friends, sweets and grandparents. They went to the lavatory and demanded to know, in carrying voices, *why* they couldn't go on their own and *what* a lurking man might do to them if they did. The girls' lavatory attendant was an old meanie – she stopped them using the green liquid soap to blow bubbles. . .

After this the poor minders had to think of other wet day activities. Nineteen seventy-seven was turning out to be cold most of the time, too cold for whole days at the river or seaside which had proved such popular pastimes during the previous year's drought. If the kids were not kept at full physical stretch all day there was trouble at bedtime. Julian and Anne, who had been kind, gentle people when they started work with us, quickly found themselves having to toughen up.

The four of them drew up a rota for bedtime duties. It looked fine on paper. All seven year olds and under, supervised by one adult, to be in bed by seven o'clock, and everyone else, supervised by a different adult, in bed by eight o'clock.

'Ha ha,' said Mary, putting the finishing touches to the bedroom list. She had drawn first watch with Julian. Mandy and Anne were off duty, watching TV with the sound turned up so that they wouldn't feel compelled to help.

By eight-thirty every single child, refreshed by a hot bath and cocoa and biscuits, was running up and down the landing. Julian was appealing to their better natures and Mary was reading *The Wind in the Willows* – to herself because nobody was listening.

Julian came in to the sitting room where Brian and I were trying to do the post. 'They're being extra difficult tonight,' he said (as if we hadn't noticed). 'Would you mind if I got them up again? I've got an idea.'

'As long as the idea is to drop them off the edge of Land's End, it's fine by me,' said Brian.

'You're on the right lines,' said Julian. 'I thought I'd take them for a cross-country run.' We stared at him.

'A run?' I said. 'But you'd have to go with them.'

'I don't mind. I'd much rather do that than argue about who's sleeping where, and hear about how they all stay up late at home.' We nodded sympathetically and he went on: 'They've not had much exercise today and it's stopped raining now. A run might tire them out.'

Julian's idea was a winner. The surprised children were stripped of their pyjamas, put in to shorts and T-shirts, and assembled in front of the house. A rumour buzzed round that it was a fire drill, then a real fire.

They jogged off happily into the dusk under the somewhat confused impression that 'the insurance' would have rebuilt the house by the time they got back.

'My brother had to get married to get a house,' said an eight-year-old from Newcastle. 'He was saving up for a Hardy fishing rod then his name came out on top of the housing list. He still hasn't got his rod.'

The evening cross-country runs became an almost daily

123

event for the insomniacs. All the children were given the choice — either go to sleep or join Julian's run. None of the other minders would go running after supper, so Julian had to put in hours of unpaid overtime. It meant that he was on bedtime duty every day except for his day off but he said he didn't mind and sometimes swapped breakfast chores to even things up.

There was one cold wet day when we had no bedtime problems. This was the day of the Queen's Silver Jubilee celebrations, an event which coincided with our changeover day, Saturday.

There were twelve morning departures to see to (three hysterical with rage at missing the village fête), eight staying on and twelve new arrivals after lunch. We worked out a plan of action. Julian and Anne would take the stayers on to the fête with a picnic lunch. Mary, Mandy and I would strip the beds, wash the sheets and clean the house while Brian saw to the collecting parents.

Then, after a cheese roll taken on the wing, we would remake the beds while we waited for the incoming children. These would be ferried to the village as soon as they arrived, and left with Julian and Anne.

When the day came our main problem (apart from exhaustion which was part and parcel of Saturdays) was getting the new children entered for the sports at the fête in time. It was one of the most confusing days imaginable.

Almost before the parents' cars had braked we whipped each small guest out of the back seat, sized him up for sports potential — we didn't want to overlook a budding Daly Thompson — and put him in Mary's car. While Brian smoothed the feathers of the parents, Mary drove down to the fête and on the way explained to the child where they were going and why. She also psyched each one up to the 500-metre or egg and spoon race or whatever. Then, having handed over to Julian and Anne, she came back for the next one.

It says a lot for the resilience of children that not only did eleven of them get to the fête dry-eyed (the twelfth was the liquid type under any circumstances) but they also enjoyed themselves no end. Our party, which was complete by 4 p.m., chalked up a creditable number of second and third prizes and even a couple of firsts.

Every child resident in the parish was given a silver crown piece and a Jubilee mug and there were bags of sweets and Union Jacks for visitors. Most of our children had already had their souvenirs at their own neighbourhood parties so there was no jealousy. The show was very well run. There were competitions for everyone from toddlers to grandads, and sideshows and music. Only the cold drizzle stopped it from being perfect. At five-thirty everything stopped for milking – a lot of small country shows in dairy areas have this charming convention – and the steward said over the tannoy that he hoped we would all be back for the evening bonfire after the milk break.

So back home we went for tea. The new children seemed to be enjoying this high-speed start to their holiday and pitched into their meal with gusto. We had pushed all the tables in the dining room together and laid out a cold buffet of chicken, ham, salad rolls and fruit.

'It's not like this every day,' said one old stager. 'We usually have to sit down and eat properly.'

'And wash,' said another, unrecognisable under a peanut-butter face mask.

'You can wash after supper instead today,' Mary said. 'We're all going back to the show tonight so you can put some warm clothes on and have a wash before you go.' Everyone groaned and wiped greasy fingers down their fronts. 'It'll be *dark*,' they said hopefully, 'and nobody's going to notice if we've washed or not.'

After supper, the three dogs were let in to the dining room to clear up the worst of the fallout. Buffet meals are enormously popular with children and it cuts down the washing up, but it does put years on the carpets.

'Aah, aren't they lovely? What are their names?' It was difficult to remember that twelve of the children had only been with us a few hours and indeed had not yet seen anything of the place other than the dining room.

'The mongrel is Honey, the spaniel is Parsley, and little bird-brain here is Ella.'

'Don't call her bird-brain, Mandy, she's lovely. We can't

have a dog, we live in a flat. Can she shake hands?'

'No, she sings though. Sing Ella, sing.' The high spot of Ella's day is when she's asked to do her party piece. She lifted her muzzle, opened her mouth and sang: 'Ooo, ooo, ooo.'

'*Ooo ooo ooo*,' echoed the children. The old house cringed and a few flakes of whitewash fluttered down from the ceiling.

'SHUT UP,' Mandy yelled. Julian said he thought the children should be allowed to shout as they were on holiday, but luckily for the state of the roof someone looked at the clock and found it was time to go.

'Listen kids,' said Brian. 'We're walking to the village tonight, it's not far and I don't want to take the van. We'll take one car for spare coats and sweaters – the old grey Mini – so have a good look at it so that you'll recognise it in the car park. Anne and Mary have got your pocket money, you can have 50p at a time.'

Mandy and I stayed behind to load the Mini with lemonade and spare clothing. It was a very cold evening and I wondered whether to make a flask of coffee.

'No, I've got a much better idea,' said Mandy. 'Is there an empty lemonade bottle?'

'Dozens. They're in a box by the freezer. Why?'

'Stay here.' She disappeared into the house while I turned the car round, and came out again with a litre lemonade bottle in a beach bag, and two tin mugs. 'Central heating,' she grinned, 'just for the two of us.'

Mandy had completed the Ten Tors walk when she was younger. This is a three-day endurance test which is part of the Duke of Edinburgh Award scheme. The youngsters are encouraged to show resourcefulness and courage in the face of physical hardship. Mandy had done her test in winter.

'Is this some concoction they taught you to make when you were camping?' I asked. She giggled to herself all the way on the drive to the village but didn't answer the question.

We parked the Mini in the churned-up field that was being used as a car park and made our way towards the lights of the show.

'There's going to be a bonfire soon,' said one of the children running towards us with an ice cream in each hand. 'Did you bring the wellies? My feet are wet already.'

'They're in the Mini, over there,' I said. 'Are you *sure* you want two ice creams so soon after supper?'

'One's for Tim.' The child vanished into the crowd. I looked at Mandy. 'Tim? Have we got a Tim?'

'No. Gosh, isn't it cold?'

'How about some of your central heating? If it's no good we can buy some coffee at the refreshment tent.'

Mandy handed me the two tin mugs and reached into the beach bag. She filled the mugs and screwed the lid back firmly on the bottle. I took a big mouthful and swallowed.

Molten lava surged down to my toenails and the Duke of Edinburgh went straight to the top of the list of my favourite men. I don't think that his award scheme specifically mentions thawing out middle-aged women at village fêtes, but perhaps they will include it in the future.

'Strewth,' I croaked, wiping tears from my eyes, 'that is *the* most delicious central heating in the world.' I drained the mug. 'What's in it?'

Mandy drank hers thoughtfully: 'It's got a basis of ginger wine,' she said.

'And?'

'And some other things. More?'

'You bet.' I held out my mug.

As the level of the bottle went down the evening became more and more enjoyable. The village elders lit the Jubilee bonfire and put foil-wrapped potatoes to bake round the bottom. Mandy and I subsided onto a pile of anoraks we were asked to 'mind' and inched back from the searing heat as the fire gained strength.

Bonfires are such companionable things. No need to talk, or even to think. Brian said we were asleep, but we couldn't have been as we both remember doing our share of nose wiping and soothing spark-frizzled fingers with Acriflavine.

Before long it was ten o'clock and Mary said she would drive the youngest children home as they were too tired to walk. 'Got the car keys?' she asked. I unzipped my anorak pocket and a landslide of plastic camels fell out. 'Our prizes,' someone explained.

'Help me to find the car keys, kids,' I said. 'They've fallen on the grass.' The children crawled around on all fours in the grass which was mined with cow pats.

Mandy rewarded the finder of the keys with a plastic camel. He said he already had four and could he have a frog instead. Mandy said in exasperation no he jolly well couldn't and would he please go and wash the cow shit off his hands.

'Where? Where do I wash?'

'The *river*,' shouted last week's children. 'Let's go to the river in the dark. What an *adventure*.'

It was a most fitting and triumphant end to a successful day. Brian and Mary took the smallest children home in the car and the rest of us, with branches taken from the bonfire, set out in a glow-worm procession along the river bank. Julian and Anne led the way, singing campfire songs, and Mandy and I shepherded from the back.

When we got to the bridge the children couldn't resist throwing their flaming torches into the river and shouting 'hooray' when the hot ends went out in a hiss of steam. The Jubilee issue of little Union Jacks came out to be waved in the dark and somebody called 'God save the Queen'.

And the Duke of Edinburgh Award scheme, I thought as I watched Mandy placidly removing a flag stick from someone's nostril.

Chapter Thirteen

ONE OF THE BOYS caught a cold as a result of the previous chilly day. While I was enlisting the aid of a six-year-old to get the top off a child-proof aspirin bottle, Mandy reached into the medicine cabinet, took out what she thought were a couple of Karvol decongestant capsules, and snipped holes in them.

'Phew, what's that pong?' Anne called out from the next room.

'Karvol,' said Mandy, rubbing it vigorously into the boy's chest.

'Karvol? That's *garlic*.' Anne came in holding her nose. 'Poor little blighter. Honestly, Faith, I don't think you should use the children for your herbal experiments. He smells like a French sailor.'

'I wouldn't know,' I said regretfully. 'And it's not my experiment. I asked Mandy to rub him with Karvol.'

The boy, a curly haired eight-year-old charmer called Malcolm, stood shivering in his vest and pants close to the Rayburn. The heat from the stove activated the garlic oil and the next child who came in recoiled as though struck and said 'Whatsa for deena?' which we thought was very witty.

'I'm awfully sorry, Malcolm,' said Mandy. 'The garlic and Karvol things look exactly the same. I didn't look at the labels.'

'Never mind,' said Malcolm kindly. 'I expect it'll wear off. Can I get dressed now?'

We rubbed him with Karvol to mask the garlic and helped him to dress. He was such an easy-going boy — the only complaint he made was that the dogs wouldn't go near him.

'Where are we going today?' The other children came in from feeding the animals. They were bright-eyed and alert expecting a repeat performance of yesterday's Jubilee celebrations.

129

'Perhaps a quiet day at home?' I suggested. 'You were all very late to bed last night.'

'Don't stay in on my account,' said Malcolm. 'I don't mind going to the seaside. It would be good for me to get some sea air, wouldn't it?' He had huge blue eyes and an air of contrived innocence that didn't fool us for a moment.

At the word 'seaside' the other children whooped with excitement and pelted upstairs for towels and swimming things. Brian came in carrying two buckets of milk. 'What's that row? And what's that *horrible* smell?'

'Garlic,' I said.

'For breakfast?' Brian shook his head and put the milk to cool in the larder. 'It'll taint the milk.' He opened all the doors and windows. The wind whipped in smartly and a row of empty yogurt pots tumbled on to the floor.

'Must you?' I shut the windows. 'It looks a bit cold to go to the seaside. In fact, I for one, flatly refuse to go.'

'Me too,' said Brian. He had been known to get seasick in the bath and I knew nothing would induce him to go mackerel fishing on a choppy sea.

'You two are *feeble*,' said Mandy. (She showed no ill effects from last night's concoction which I now knew had included nearly a pint of whisky.) 'We'll take them on our own.' The others, who seemed to have forgotten the cinema episode, nodded agreement.

'Eight childless hours,' Brian murmured, shutting his eyes and savouring the moment. My mind leapt forward. Rolls, cheese, fruit, coffee, Savlon, Elastoplast, damp flannels, pocket money. . .

Half an hour later a picnic lunch for twenty-four was secured firmly in the boot of one of the cars. Anne and Mary had brought their own cars with them and could take five children in each. Julian drove the Mini van with Mandy in the passenger seat and ten children sardined in the back.

At 10 a.m. we waved the convoy goodbye. 'See you at six o'clock, be good, 'bye.' We went indoors and made plans over a cup of coffee, parcelling out the precious hours carefully.

'I'll take the dogs for a walk,' Brian said, 'and buy the Sunday papers on the way back.'

'And I'll take Monty and go for a ride,' I said, naming a place we knew where wild herbs attracted some quite rare butterflies. There were orchids too, growing in the same area and we felt privileged to have discovered it.

We shut the door on the chaos in the kitchen. Once, ages ago, some friends had dropped in when we were out, and had cleaned the place up to pass the time while they waited for us. They left before we got back. This reinforced our belief in fairies and we are ever optimistic that if we leave the key in the door it might happen again. Brian whistled the dogs to heel and set out.

I saddled Monty and rode off a few minutes later, trying not to listen to the envious calls of the other ponies. Monty was the natural choice for a 'quiet' ride. He was the only one who would stand still for any length of time if I wanted to watch wild birds or animals.

Monty and I didn't stay out long because it was too windy to stand around in the orchid place and the few butterflies that were out looked quite frostbitten. We trotted home, stopping off at Ursula's on the way for a cup of coffee.

I think Ursula was more pleased to see Monty than me. Her grass needed cutting. 'Can't you leave him here for the day?' she asked when I got up to go. 'He's much better than that wretched Flymo thing.'

'Yes, all right. We're not using any of the ponies today. Do you want Wellington too? They'd get it cleared quite quickly between them.'

'Could I really have two? That would be splendid.'

Wellington thought it was splendid too and did a few circuits round the grass directly he was released in the garden. Ursula cursed him with a surprisingly vivid turn of phrase and told him what she'd do to his beastly feet if he didn't cut it out.

I walked home and found Brian finishing the washing up. 'Lousy fairies are on strike again,' he grumbled.

We lit a fire in the sitting room and took food and papers in. Brian had bought both the *Observer* and *Sunday Times*, for a treat. For the rest of the afternoon the only sounds to be heard were the rustle of papers and contented sighs of the dogs as they toasted themselves on the fireside rug.

By milking time storm clouds were gathering and the wind was bending the bean poles to and fro.

'This isn't going to do the pansies any good,' Brian said. 'Some of the seed pods were nearly ripe yesterday. I was thinking of harvesting them soon.' We milked Elizabeth and fed the pigs, rabbits and poultry, then went to have a look.

The crop looked beautiful. We had followed the seed firm's instructions and removed the 'rogue' pansies — any which were not blue — so that the remaining ones were a solid block of deep blue. About half of them had finished the first flowering and the seed pods were ripening well. Some had already split and the wind had spilled the seeds on to the ground.

'What a waste.' Brian shook his head in annoyance. 'I don't think we'll get any from this flowering unless the wind drops. No wonder pansy seed is so dear if a bit of wind can affect it like this. Perhaps we should have gone in for lupins or hollyhocks.'

'Perhaps. Anyway they'll flower again soon so we'll just keep our fingers crossed that the weather will improve. I'd better get Monty and Wellie back from Ursula's now, before it rains.'

I met our three cars coming along the road and the children spotted me before I could dive in to a hedge.

'She's got *halters*!' they screamed. 'Take me, take me, take me.' I put my hands over my ears.

'I'll take Malcolm.' I said. Malcolm was out of Anne's car in a flash and I grabbed his hand and hurried on, with the strain of 'It's not *fair*' getting fainter and fainter.

'Where are we going?' asked Malcolm.

'I lent a couple of ponies to a friend and we're going to ride them home bareback. Have you had a nice day?'

'Lovely, thank you. We've been mackerel fishing and in the arcades. Nearly everyone swam but Mary said I wasn't to because of my cold.'

'I guessed that. That's why you're coming with me to have a pony ride.'

'Oh, I wondered why you chose me. It's nice being chosen, isn't it? It must be awful to be someone who gets picked last for team games and things, mustn't it? May I carry one of the halters, please? I'll be Red Rum. Who are you?'

'I'll be Stroller.'

Ursula met us at her garden gate and shook hands with Red Rum. 'You're the chap who caught a chill, aren't you?' she said. 'Wasn't it a good bonfire last night?'

'Last night?' Malcolm tried to remember the Jubilee fête. 'I say, was it only last night? It seems ages ago.' Ursula looked at his flushed face and bunged-up nose.

'Have you still got that jar of goose grease I gave you, Faith?' she asked. 'It's supposed to be very good for chesty colds.'

'My cold is much better thank you,' Malcolm said hurriedly. He looked at the sky. 'We'd better hurry or we'll get caught in the rain.'

Ursula and I laughed and took the hint. We lifted him on to Wellington's back and gave him the end of the halter-rope to hold.

'How do I steer?' he asked.

'You don't have to. The ponies know their own way home. All we have to do is sit on their backs and enjoy the ride.'

Monty and Wellie plodded home, their bellies satisfyingly full of Ursula's lawn. When we dismounted they licked Malcolm's hands which made him laugh.

'Why do they do that?' he asked.

'They like the taste of the salt on your skin. They can probably tell you've been to the seaside.'

'In olden days people couldn't buy salt. Did you know that? We did it in history.'

'M'm, I know.'

'Salt was so precious they sometimes swapped it for things instead of money. Do you suppose that's why gentlemen used to kiss ladies' hands? To get the salt?'

'It hadn't occurred to me, no. You could be right.'

Someone banged the gong indoors. Malcolm wiped his saliva-coated hands on Monty's neck and did the four-minute mile to the dining room.

I marvelled at his energy. In fact the energy of the whole group was phenomenal. They had already taken Lyme Regis by the throat and squeezed every drop of entertainment value

133

from it. They had been swimming and mackerel fishing before lunch, then fossil hunting and castle building afterwards. Rain had driven them into an amusement arcade for an hour and when it had stopped they all went back to the beach and played French cricket. They had hired paddle-boats, jumped on trampolines, dug a hole to Australia and raced each other to the end of the Cob and back. (The Cob is Lyme's famous harbour jetty.)

Now, fortified by roast chicken and blackberry and apple pie, they seemed set for an energetic evening. They built a fort of floor cushions in the playroom and defended it with pillows. Julian went in to tell them it was bedtime and came out again covered in feathers. 'I think I need reinforcements,' he laughed. 'I'm outnumbered.'

Anne and Mandy went to help him. Mary and I shut the kitchen door and washed up the dinner things. Even with the door shut, we could hear the racket clearly.

'Pick up all these feathers *at once*.'

'That's Mandy,' Mary grinned, 'on the warpath.'

Julian tried next. His was a calm reasonable approach. The only result he got was well-aimed Womble. 'Ouch,' we heard him say. 'Who threw that Womble?'

Suddenly there was a sound like rifle fire, and all the lights flickered.

'I think Brian's shooting them,' Mary said calmly.

'He'd do anything to watch the nine o'clock news in peace,' I agreed. A flash of lightning lit up the sky and almost immediately another thunderclap followed.

'A storm!' The children poured into the kitchen, shrill with excitement.

Mary, quick to see an easy way of getting them to bed, grabbed a few and aimed them towards the stairs. 'Up you go, quickly children. We'll have a much better view from the bedroom windows.'

Within minutes everyone was in pyjamas and dressing-gowns, jostling for position in the deep window-seats of their bedrooms.

The storm stayed right overhead for a while. There was sheet lightning and forked lightning and bang after bang of deafening thunder. When it eventually rumbled away towards Taunton, the children climbed off the window-seats and got into bed. Ten minutes later they were all asleep.

'That storm was very well organised, Brian, if I may say so,' said Julian. 'I didn't know how we were going to get them off tonight.'

'It wasn't easy,' said Brian. 'I had to grease a few palms at top level.'

We finished washing up and took a tray of tea through to the sitting room. Julian, Anne and Mary pounced on the Sunday papers and settled back with pig-like grunts of contentment. Mandy entertained us with the story of how Anne failed to catch a mackerel.

'Her line got caught round the propeller under the fishing boat, didn't it, Anne?'

'Why don't you go and top up the teapot, big mouth?'

Mandy laughed: 'Oh, come on Anne, I know it was embarrassing at the time but you must admit it was funny.'

'What was funny?' I asked.

'Well, the fisherman switched off the engine and tried to untangle the line, but it was wound round and round the propeller blades and it wouldn't budge. And the boat was bobbing around like mad — the sea was really choppy today — so the children's lines got crossed. It was like a cat's cradle. Then the fisherman got his tin trumpet thing out and shouted to one of the other fishing boats to go back and call the breakdown boat out.'

'Like the AA?'

'Yes and no. The breakdown boat really only helps people in trouble, like sinking or drowning or something serious. They weren't too pleased to find it was just some twit fouling the propeller.'

'Thanks,' muttered Anne.

'But the best bit was the rescue men's faces when they saw the kids. Half of them were being seasick — the kids I mean — because the boat was bucketing up and down and they'd all had their usual Coke/candy floss/hamburger snacks before lunch. . .'

'OK. OK. Don't spell it out,' said Brian.

'And the ones that weren't being sick were pretending it was Trafalgar and saying "Kiss me Hardy" and dying all over the seats. They didn't want to be towed in, did they, Anne? They hadn't had the full hour.'

'Why did the rescue people tow you in? Couldn't they mend the propeller either?'

'The man didn't even ask them to. He just wanted to get back to the beach.'

'Sensible chap,' said Brian. 'You'd better give Lyme Regis a miss for a while.'

'Are there any other beaches where we can hire boats, Mandy?' Anne asked.

'There's Beer,' said Mandy. 'I prefer Beer to Lyme, it's never as crowded and the parking is a lot easier.'

'Beer it is then,' said Brian, 'but let's keep them at home for a couple of days. They've already had the fête and a day at Lyme. That's enough outings to be going on with.'

The children thought otherwise. They enjoyed the farm activities well enough but the weather continued to be cold and wet and once they had had their pony rides there just wasn't enough to occupy them out of doors. The minders organised indoor games – treasure hunts, charades and so forth – but these didn't mop up a fraction of the children's energy.

'Can't we stop feeding them?' Anne suggested. It was Wednesday lunchtime and the children had chomped their way through a catering pack of 144 sausage rolls, 5 lb of grilled tomatoes and two gallons of custard with bananas. They scraped their dishes clean, put the dirty crockery on the kitchen trolley and waited expectantly for a grown-up to announce the next game on the agenda.

'Give us a chance kids,' Julian begged. 'Go and do something restful for half an hour while we have our coffee.'

'What are we going to do this afternoon?' they asked. Julian looked out of the window. The rain was coming down steadily and the sky was metallic.

'Can we go to the beach?'

'Of course you can't go to the beach, nitwit. It's pelting down,' said Julian.

'It's nice, swimming in the rain.'

136

'Swimming,' said Mandy. 'How about that Sports Centre in Wellington? We could take them to the indoor pool this afternoon.'

The Sports Centre proved to be our salvation. As well as the pool there were badminton courts, table-tennis tables, a gym and hot showers, all staffed with adult attendants who absorbed our twenty without turning a hair.

'Why couldn't we have come here before?' said Mandy. 'It's the answer to a minder's prayer.'

'We haven't had such lousy weather before. Not for days on end. Don't forget the kids are supposed to be getting a farm holiday, not outings every day.'

On Thursday it rained again and the children voted unanimously for another trip to the Sports Centre. Brian drove them there in the morning, then he and I were able to get a half-day SHA meeting before collecting them at teatime.

The weather improved on Friday. It wasn't sunny and there was a stiffish breeze but at least it didn't rain. After the children had had their rides they begged to go to the beach for a last day treat.

'It's been treat after treat all week,' said Julian. 'You haven't stayed at home for a single day.'

'Oh go on, Julian, be a sport. How about Lyme Regis?'

'We'll take you to Beer,' Mandy said. 'But only for a couple of hours. Most of you have got to get packed ready to go home tomorrow.'

The children pushed aside this dismal thought and asked Brian if there would be a bonfire.

'I doubt it,' he said, 'after all this rain there won't be any dry wood.'

'Perhaps we could find some bits of driftwood on the beach this afternoon,' Mandy suggested. Brian looked at her.

'He doesn't want to have a bonfire, twerp,' I whispered, 'it's ankle deep in mud everywhere.' Mandy hastily amended 'driftwood' to 'shells'.

'We'll go shell hunting on the beach at Beer, eh kids?'

Unhappily, the joys of shell hunting palled for six of the kids, and by a simple trick they slipped away from the beach group and went shoplifting in town.

We were stunned.

'It *can't* be,' Brian said. 'Not shoplifting, damn it, they're only nine years old.'

It was later in the evening and the children were getting ready for bed. Brian and Julian, checking through the pocket-money notebook discovered some discrepancies. Six of the children seemed to have bought expensive presents for their parents in Beer and, as they had drawn only 50p each that day, something was evidently fishy.

'Let's not jump the gun,' I said. 'There may be another explanation. Perhaps they've been saving their money for one final binge on their last day.'

'But they haven't,' Julian said. 'I've been doing the pocket-money book nearly every day this week. All the kids have drawn up to their limits and I've seen the things they've been buying on other days. Here, see for yourself.'

The pocket-money notebook was neatly marked off in columns. Against each child's name was the amount he had brought with him and handed into our safekeeping on arrival. In the next six columns – the days of the week – were entered the amounts he had drawn from his account. Every Friday night the children who were going home on Saturday were given back any money owing to them.

The six under suspicion had started the week with £5 each. (This was the amount we suggested to the parents when they came, and give or take a pound, it was about normal.) According to the notebook they had each spent £2.50 at the Jubilee fête and 50p a day since then. Even if they had saved all their money it wouldn't explain how they came to have boxes of chocolates, scent, cigarettes, fountain pens and, incredibly, a man's tweed cap.

'Let's start at the beginning,' I said. 'Who has actually seen these presents?'

'All the loot's on the chests of drawers in their rooms,' Mandy said. 'It's not hidden. They've been comparing notes.'

'Don't say loot,' Brian snapped.

'I'll go and fetch it all down here,' said Mandy.

'I'll help you,' said Julian. He and Mandy went upstairs. Brian paced up and down the room and I stared unseeingly out of the window.

In a couple of minutes Julian and Mandy were back and dumped the suspect goods on the settee. Julian picked up a pencil and totted up the approximate value of everything.

'Hell,' he said. 'I make it about forty pounds. What are we going to do?'

'I'll get the kids down,' I said. 'There *must* be an explanation.'

But there wasn't. The six nine-year-olds admitted their crime; bandied around words like 'nicked' and 'pinched' and seemed genuinely surprised that we regarded thieving as thieving and not as a high-spirited prank.

'What a fuss about a few pickings,' said one. Mandy fetched him a stinging smack that made his eyes water and told him to mind his manners.

Brian lectured them about dishonesty, first in general terms then from the viewpoint of a small shopkeeper. It went in one ear and out of the other — there wasn't much in between to stop it — and was a depressing experience. When they had been sent to bed, Brian said he felt like cancelling the remainder of the holiday bookings.

On a more practical note, Julian and Mandy offered to take the stolen items back to Beer the next day.

'I know a lot of shopkeepers and stallholders at Beer,' Mandy said. 'I think I'll be able to find which shops the stuff came from.'

'And we'd better not go to Beer with next week's kids in case we get arrested for receiving,' I said.

'We could start a protection racket,' Mandy suggested with a grin. 'Get the fisherman at Lyme and shopkeepers at Beer to pay us to keep the kids away.'

'Let's forget it,' Brian said. 'They'll be gone tomorrow. Let's have some music.' He leafed through a pile of records, ignoring shafts of wit from the minders (on the level of 'Wind it up, Brian' and 'How about "Maid of the Mountains"?') He put a Louis Armstrong on and turned the sound up. 'I know you'd probably prefer David Bowie or Throbbing Boil,' he said, 'but since I've only got good music you may as well learn to like it. We'll have Louis and Ella, then more Louis.'

Chapter Fourteen

SARA PHONED on Sunday.

'Guess what? Gerry and I have got the caretaking job. We start in two weeks' time. Seventy pounds a week, use of car, free electricity and free phone.'

'Free phone? They must be mad.'

'They're foreign and *rolling*. Honestly, you've never seen anything like it. They've got Rolls Royces and –'

'Plural?'

'Yes, plural. It's two families actually. The husbands are in business together and they've bought this country estate in Sussex between them for weekends. They've got phones in the cars and genuine Picassos.'

'That *is* ostentatious.'

'Not in the cars, stupid, in one of their flats. It's one of those posh addresses in Eaton Square. There are electronic beams to stop burglars and three dobermans.'

'Three? What have they got, the crown jewels?'

'They didn't mean to have three. They bought one and it turned out to be diabetic, so they went back to the breeder for another one and he told them that the only two he had left for sale were inseparable. So they bought both. Are you still there?'

'Yes. I'm lost in admiration for the breeder's sales technique. I wish I'd thought of that one.'

'The joke is that all three are useless. They licked us to bits when we walked in, they don't seem to have a clue about guarding. Anyway, what I'm really phoning for is to say would it be OK if Gerry and I came down on Tuesday to see you? We'd like to stay overnight if there's room.'

'There aren't any beds but one of you could have the settee and there are plenty of floor cushions in the playroom. Tuesday would be fine, we're taking them to a show in the morning but you won't be here early, will you?'

'No, we'll probably get there about supper time. What are they like this week? Any more crooks?'

'No, thank goodness. Mandy and Julian returned all the stuff yesterday morning and promised the shopkeepers it wouldn't happen again. The kids this week are mainly repeat bookings from last year. We've got three weird ones though. I'll tell you about them on Tuesday.'

The weird children I had mentioned to Sara were a weepy ten-year-old called Suzanne, and two sisters, Abigail and Felicity.

Suzanne's father was a very nice man, full of apologies for his dreary daughter. 'She comes from a long line of snivellers,' he said. 'Her mother, grandmother and aunts, they all cry at the drop of a hat. It's only fair to tell you that she doesn't want to come, but honestly I must have a couple of weeks' peace.'

Brian and I looked at Suzanne without enthusiasm. She had fair, almost white, hair, pointed features and red-rimmed eyes. (Mandy used to call her the albino weasel.) She held a soggy handkerchief to her face and looked at her parents beseechingly: 'Won't you change your mind *please*, sniff sniff. Don't make me stay here. Mum, please make Dad take me with you.'

Her mother had a rather frozen face, like someone who has been given bad news. She was all for siding with Suzanne, but her husband, who plainly was at the end of his tether with the pair of them, stood up to go. Mother and daughter clung together, and mingled tears.

'*Christ*, will you give it a rest, Suzanne?' He turned to Brian and handed him a piece of paper: 'Here's our holiday address until next Saturday. We'll be at home for the second week. She'll probably want to keep phoning us but I'd sooner she didn't. I can't tell you what it means to us to get away on our own.'

'Has Suzanne been away from you before?' I asked. 'She seems very dependent on you.'

'She's been to relatives and to one other holiday place last year. She didn't like going but then she doesn't like anything. She cries at school, then she comes home and cries at home. My wife's mother lives with us and you should see the three of them if there's a weepy on television. If I didn't have my greenhouse I'd be in an asylum.'

At the mention of greenhouse Brian stopped looking glumly at Suzanne and carted her father off to admire the sweetpeas and commiserate over the pansies. Mrs Sniveller sat in their car and I took Suzanne upstairs to show her her bedroom.

I must admit that I have no time at all for children who use tears as a weapon, and if mine had tried it on I should have given them something to cry about long before they reached Suzanne's age. But you can't clout other people's children. I dumped her case in her room and told her to put her clothes in a chest of drawers.

'The bathroom's at the end of the landing. When you've unpacked, go and wash your face and someone will show you round.' Mary and Anne were just finishing making the beds before rushing off to meet a train and they looked up and whispered: 'Is she homesick?'

'No, just a pain in the neck. Where's Mandy?'

'She's doing labels for the bedroom doors. There are fifteen boys and only five girls this week so we thought we'd put all the girls in here together.'

Suzanne's face brightened a little when she heard there were to be fifteen boys and my opinion of her rose a few notches. Nobody's hopeless while they've still got their hormones intact.

'Do you like boys, Suzanne?'

She shrugged. 'Don't know any.'

'Aren't there any boys at your school?'

'No, it's all girls.'

Ho hum, I thought, no *wonder* you've been crying all these years. A manless world, how awful. I whizzed downstairs two at a time to tell Brian I had solved Suzanne's problem and crashed into a mountain of luggage at the foot of the stairs.

'What twit put this – oh, er, hullo.' Brian was bringing in a newly arrived family. SOS signals were pouring out of his head.

'This is my wife,' he said, in such a relieved voice they must have thought I'd been wrestling with alligators upstairs. 'Mr and Mrs West and Abigail and Felicity.'

Abigail and Felicity aged ten and eleven, were a credit to their taxidermist, they were almost lifelike.

'They're nervous, poor souls,' Mrs West explained when I failed to get a flicker out of either them. She had a plummy voice and her outfit was more Knightsbridge than Marks and Spencer's which in some way made their story all the more extraordinary.

For Mrs West had won a raffle and the prize was a week for two in somewhere hot.

'And it's not as though I'm the sort to go in for raffles,' she said apologetically, as if raffles were on a par with coal in the bath and Saturday-night sex. 'We went to a fund-raising dinner and dance. For the Party, you understand, so it was all in a good cause.'

'So you're off for an exotic week then?' I said, before Brian could start educating them. Thank goodness he wasn't sporting his little badge with the slogan Don't Blame Me I Voted Labour.

'Well, of course. One couldn't waste it, could one? But we simply can't risk taking the girls. They *collapse* in the sun, don't you darlings? We wintered in the Bahamas once and my dear, *never* again. I *lived* at the chemist – *pints* of calamine, don't you know?'

We didn't. Brian told them that we used to winter in Muswell Hill and they laughed like anything – I really don't think they saw he was pulling their legs.

There were more parents due soon so Brian and I nudged them towards the bottom of the stairs. The girls stuck close to their father and looked blank when we handed them some of their luggage to carry up.

'Leave it for the staff, girls,' the father ordered. The girls dropped the cases like well-trained gun dogs.

'Real leather,' I said admiringly. 'Doesn't it smell nice?' Four blank looks greeted this remark. I suppose all one's luggage was leather if one wintered in the Bahamas.

'Will you excuse me? I think there are some more cars

arriving,' Brian said, and vanished. The family followed me up the stairs, along the landing and into the girls' bedroom.

'*Five* beds?' said Mrs West, kneading a mattress vigorously.

'Yes. There are only five girls this week so we've put them all together. More fun for them, don't you think?'

No she didn't. Oh hell. Whose stupid idea was it to run a guest house anyway?

.'This simply *won't* do at all, Mrs Addis. I made it clear on the booking form that the girls were to have a double room with a private bathroom. And this is so . . . so basic.'

She nearly said primitive. I looked round the room, and tried to see it through her eyes. The walls were freshly emulsioned in white, with the lovely old beams left as the builders of three hundred years ago had intended. The window, set in a two-foot-thick recess, was curtained with a floral cotton print and this was echoed on the bedspreads. There was a handbasin, sparkling clean because it was Saturday, a fitted carpet ditto, and three chests of drawers in stripped pine. Yes, it was basic. Basically very nice indeed.

I started to remind her that I had written to her about the shared sleeping arrangements (we kept the double rooms for very young children or bedwetters), when I noticed that Abigail and Felicity were both shivering with fright. This wasn't a put on act like Suzanne's but the real thing. I put an arm round each of them.

'Please don't be frightened,' I said. 'Are you worried about sharing a room?' They nodded.

'I can't conjure up a private bathroom,' I said to Mrs West, 'but I will put them in a small double room as they're so nervous.'

'I'd like to see it, please,' said Mrs West. They trooped along the landing after me. Several small boys cannoned into us.

'Wotcha,' said a familiar voice.

'Craig! Garry!' Two favourites from last year. 'Gosh, it's good to see you.' I gave them a hug. 'How's Munchie, Craig?' (Munchie was Craig's rabbit, a souvenir from his holiday at Phyllishayes last year.)

Craig grinned. 'Pregnant again. Did you get me Christmas card?'

'Yes thanks. How many did she have in her last litter?'

'Five. They do breed like flippin rabbits, don't they?'

Mrs West gave a gasp of horror and I remembered I was supposed to be showing them the girls' bedroom.

'See you later, lads, I'm busy now.'

'Take your time. We've met Mandy and Julian and they told us to put our stuff in our old room. S'lot cleaner'n last year, ain't it?'

'We've got water now.' And under my breath: '*Hop it.*' They looked at Abigail and Felicity understandingly, winked at each other and continued on their way.

'A couple of boys from last year,' I explained, and before Mrs West could say anything about not wanting her daughters to mix with the hoi polloi, we collided with, of all people, Mrs Pearce and Quentin coming out of a bedroom. Julian was hosting them. There was no sign of Quentin's medical notebook and Julian looked reasonably relaxed.

I said hullo to Mrs Pearce and Quentin then said apologetically to Julian: 'Could you rearrange the boys' bedrooms? I need this one for these two girls.'

'I thought all the girls were going to be in together. I've put Quentin in here with Malcolm.'

'Yes, I know, I'm sorry. But these two had better have it.'

Julian looked at the trembling girls and nodded: 'Right you are. Come on, Quentin, let's find a couple of other places for you and Malcolm.'

Mrs Pearce said Quentin had been looking forward to sleeping in the same room he had had at Easter, but Mrs West steamed past her and sat firmly on one of the beds.

People who talk of 'Monday morning' feeling should try running a guest house. Monday mornings are non-starters compared to Saturday afternoons. You have been up at daybreak and coped with meals, washing, house cleaning and tearful departing guests. You have thrown a houseplant at the phone to stop it ringing, and tripped over dogs, cats and suitcases. By 2 p.m. you are at your lowest ebb and all you long for is a full mug of coffee and a hot bath. Then the new parents arrive . . .

Sail gave way to steam and Mrs Pearce gathered up Quentin's things and followed Julian out.

'Could you ask Garry and Craig to bring up the suitcases at the bottom of the stairs please, Julian?' I called after him.

Mr West joined Abigail and Felicity at the window. 'Splendid views eh, darlings? You'll have some grand gallops round those fields.' He was an amiable clot of a man and shortsighted too if he thought you could gallop round a field full of milking Friesians.

'They're not our fields actually,' I said. 'Ours are on the other side of the house. Do you like riding, girls?'

The girls nodded. 'They've been riding since they were four,' said Mrs West. 'They go to a *very* good place every Saturday.' She named one of the second string Royals whose children also took riding lessons there and I grabbed at this conversational lifeline. Anything was better than having her running down the furniture again.

Garry and Craig staggered in with the girls' luggage.

'Blinking heavy these are, what you got in there, bricks?' said Garry.

'Thank you very much boys. Is that the lot?'

Felicity and Abigail stayed mute. Garry and Craig sat down on the bed, one on each side of Mrs West. She looked rather silly sitting there with her Janet Reger petticoat showing, and trying to make herself shrink so that she didn't come into contact with them.

'There's a girl crying in the end room,' said Garry conversationally. 'I told her to put a sock in it.'

'Boys, *please*,' I said, 'fetch the rest of the suitcases then go and help someone else.'

They muttered something about slave-drivers and went out, leaving the door open. Mandy and Anne had returned from collecting some boys from the station and noisy reunions were taking place outside the lavatory.

'It's OK to pull the chain this year, isn't it?'

'Hullo Lee, hi Rupert.'

'You going to be in there all day thingy?'

'Who's in there?'

'Stephen.'

'Oh good, I didn't know he was coming this year, I thought he was too old. How old are you, Steve?'

'Twelve and a quarter.'

'THAT'S TOO OLD. YOU HAVE TO BE UNDER TWELVE.'

'Stop shouting. I was under twelve when we made the booking.'

'Hurry up, Steve, I'm busting for a pee. Hullo, what's your name?'

'Malcolm. I came last week. Why don't you use the downstairs loo?'

Mrs West was growing more and more uptight, and I knew I should be biting chunks out of the woodwork if she started up again. I said I had things to see to, and closed the door behind me as I left.

Mandy broke up the lavatory party. Malcolm wrapped himself round her legs and said he didn't want to change bedrooms in case it made him feel insecure.

'Insecure? You? Who have you been talking to?'

'Quentin's mother,' Malcolm giggled, and then in a falsetto voice: 'Quentin's liable to have nightmares if he feels insecure. I *do* think he should stay in the same bedroom, young man.'

'Young man?'

'Julian. She called Julian young man. Isn't she funny? Julian finished growing a long time ago.'

'Where is she, Mandy?' I asked.

'Outside. She wanted to see you before she left but Julian's coping. The notebook's back you'll be pleased to hear. Eyestrain is the latest fad.'

'Eyestrain? I thought it was insecurity.'

'No, eyestrain. Will you get off my legs, Malcolm, you pest.'

'Can I have a piggy-back down the stairs?'

Mandy hoisted him on to her back and we went downstairs to have a head count.

'Eighteen. Just two to come,' I said, looking at the list by the phone. Mandy made a pot of tea and we carried it out to Elizabeth's milking stall so that we could recharge our batteries in peace while the others saw to departing cars. Not that Malcolm needed recharging but he cheered us up with more impersonations of Quentin's mother and we were pleased to have him around.

'What are we going to do about the West parents?' Mandy asked.

'I don't know. They're a long time saying goodbye, aren't they? I've got to go and start cooking the dinner in a minute. If I shut the kitchen door could you manage to hoof them out through the front door?'

'What if they want to see you?'

'Tell them I've died, anything. Use your imagination.'

'I could tell them you're a drug addict and you're having a fix.'

'They'd probably believe you. No, I know. Tell them I'm seeing to some other parents.'

'There aren't any cars here.'

'They walked. They came by ox cart. Use your *loaf*.'

Malcolm came with me and I sat him at the kitchen table to shell peas. We were having roast lamb, roast potatoes, runner beans, peas, and apple pie and cream to follow. Malcolm didn't think he would be able to shell all the peas on his own so he brought in cack-handed Quentin to help him.

'I've improved since Easter,' Quentin assured me when he saw that I was not jumping for joy at the prospect of him helping. 'After all, I'm older now. I've discovered all sorts of things I couldn't do before.'

'Such as? Can you tie your own shoelaces? Button your shirt in the right holes?'

'Sometimes I can if I have long enough. But what I *can* do is write plays.'

'You what?'

'Write plays. I'm good at it. Mummy says I'll get eyestrain if I do too many, but I enjoy it.'

'What do you mean "too many"? How many have you written?'

'Thirty-one.'

I stared at him, speechless. *Thirty-one*?

'Only one act each,' he said modestly. 'My hand gets tired.'

Chapter Fifteen

IT DIDN'T SEEM a very promising start to the week. Three weirdies and an embryonic Chekhov is not a mix anyone but perhaps the real Chekhov would choose.

We welcomed in the last two arrivals, sisters called Fern and Briony. Nice uncomplicated kids they were, bred from nice uncomplicated parents, who didn't win raffles or instil hypochondria in their children. The fifteen boys, most of whom had been before, punched each others' heads for the privilege of showing Fern and Briony round, and boasted about their exploits of the previous year.

By suppertime everyone bar Suzanne, Abigail and Felicity had made friends. Suzanne had taken one look at her fellow guests and decided to add boys to the long list of things she didn't like. (So much for your stupid theory, Brian had said.) She grew bored crying in her bedroom without an audience so she went and sat in the playroom where some of the others were watching television.

Nine-year-old Rupert, who was very soft-hearted and a lady-killer into the bargain, put his arm round her and offered her a piece of chewing gum. She took his chewing gum but spurned his advances. Rupert was confused by this double insult and appealed to Julian: 'That's not *fair*, is it, Julian? I only wanted to cuddle her.'

Julian, who privately thought that anyone who wanted to cuddle Suzanne needed his head testing, had a tactful man to man chat with Rupert, pointing out that not all girls like to be cuddled, especially on so short an acquaintance. He was literally saved by the gong from having to be more explicit about female psychology.

'Dinner time,' he said. 'Go and wash your hands and sit up at the table.' He went upstairs to fetch Abigail and Felicity and came down without them.

'They won't come down,' he said, 'they want their dinner taken up.'

'I'll go,' Mary said. Anne and Mandy and I served the food while Julian kept order in the dining room, then Mary reappeared with Abigail and Felicity. They were clutching each other for support and looking fixedly at their feet.

'They're scared stiff,' Mary whispered. 'I had a hell of a job to get them out of their room.'

The other children glanced incuriously at their strange companions and continued putting away their meat and two veg at a rate of knots. Abigail and Felicity picked at their food and, as soon as they could, bolted back to their bedroom.

'I suppose I'd better take them some books and games if they're determined to be anti-social,' I said.

Mary laughed. 'Haven't you seen the stuff they've brought with them? I don't think they need any more.'

'What have they got?'

'It would be quicker for you to go and see than for me to tell you. I'd better warn you though — they've brought their own sheets and pillowcases.'

'I don't mind. Anything for less washing.'

'You'll mind the reason. Apparently Mummy says it's best not to take chances with germs. What do you make of that?'

'It's insulting. But wouldn't it save time on Saturdays if everyone brought sheets? I think I could swallow quite a few insults if it saved work.'

I was surprised to find what else they had brought. A large transistor radio, board games, books, playing cards, art materials and stationery, and boxes and boxes of sweets, biscuits and crisps.

'Crikey girls, you certainly are all set for a siege, aren't you?' I said, looking round their room. I put their suitcases on top of the wardrobe to give them more floor space, and as I did so the wardrobe door flew open. Inside there were more boxes of confectionery and three dozen cans of fizzy drinks.

'No wonder your luggage was so heavy. You didn't need to bring this, you know. In fact I don't see how you can possibly get through this lot in a week.'

'Daddy said it would be nice to have tuck boxes,' whispered

Abigail. 'He said he was always jolly glad of his at boarding school because the food wasn't very good.'

As it was their first night and they were still paralytic at the strangeness of being away from home I didn't pursue the matter. I asked them not to play their radio and said good-night.

But the next day I dropped a hint to one of the youngest boys that there might be good things to be had if he played his cards right with Abigail and Felicity. Within the hour the tomtoms were throbbing.

'How do you know?'

'What *is* it?'

'Who's got it?'

With the subtlety of a sledgehammer my little grass told all. 'It's something beginning with toffees and those quiet girls have got lots.'

It's extremely difficult to be a recluse with eighteen of your peers swarming in your bedroom, but Abigail and Felicity managed it. They shared their 'tuck' — whether willingly or not we never knew — and when it was all gone, firmly resisted any further invasions into their privacy.

The only activity in which they took part was riding. They had been well taught and rode superbly, but once the ride was over they retreated back to their room. There was no point in forcing them to join in so we let them be. They spent their time washing their smalls, writing to their pen friends and reading. As one of the other kids said — what a waste of a holiday.

We had intended spending half a day at an agricultural show on Tuesday but when the day came it was so hot and sunny we decided to stay out until suppertime. Abigail and Felicity wouldn't come so Julian and Anne offered to stay at home and count it as their day off.

There was a rodeo competition at the show and Mandy intended to win it. We told her she had to maintain the honour of the house as one of our minders had won the women's section the previous year. To her fury the rules had been changed this year. Men and women were to compete on equal terms.

'Bloody Women's Lib!' she stormed. 'It's crazy. They can't

expect girls to do as well as men in a rodeo.'

'But when you become a jockey you'll have to race against men,' I said.

'That's different. Racing's not a test of strength. This is as stupid as having a tug-of-war competition between men and women. I'll be able to stay on for five or ten seconds but I bet you anything the men do about twenty.'

Her prediction was spot on. She rode her bronco for eight seconds, beating her female opponents by a clear two seconds, but all the men stayed on for at least fifteen and the winner clocked up twenty-two.

But nothing keeps Mandy down for long. She tucked her shirt back into her jeans and, while the adrenalin was still flowing, marched off to win prizes for rifle shooting, bowling and coconut shying.

'*More* goldfish?' Brian said. He and I are also dab hands at accurate aiming and had won quite a collection of fairground nasties ourselves.

'Don't be such a wet blanket,' Mandy said. She transferred her fourth goldfish into a large jar brought along for the purpose. 'It's better than all those horrible gnomes and dogs you keep winning.'

The children homed in on the van at lunchtime. They had been on a balloon-buying spree and wanted to know where they could put them while they ate their picnic. Brian bunched all the strings together and gave them to a boy called Stephen, who'd been with us last year, to hold while he went to look for a longer piece of string. Stephen looked at the eighteen gas-filled balloons and was seized with what he called an inspiration.

'I'll be back soon,' he called, and ran towards the showground entrance holding the balloons aloft.

The other children climbed on top of the van and munched cold chicken and sausages.

'See that man over there — the one in a uniform — he lives in a kennel.'

'In a kennel? How do you know?'

'They said so over the loudspeaker. He was leading the foxhounds round the ring.'

'Not in *a* kennel, cretin,' Mandy laughed. 'He's a hunt servant, he lives in kennels.'

'What does that mean?'

'He looks after the foxhounds. He has a house next door to the kennels.'

The children lost interest in the man. There wasn't anything special about him if he didn't live in a kennel. Then two cars caught their attention. They had stuck bumper to bumper and their wheels whistled as the cars threshed backwards and forwards, locked in combat.

'Throw a bucket of cold water over them,' shouted Garry. Eventually four burly farmers lifted the cars clear of each other and the free entertainment was over.

Stephen returned, balloonless. 'I sold them,' he said proudly, 'got a penny profit on each.'

'*Stephen*. That was very naughty,' I said. 'You're not allowed to buy and sell things at a fair.'

'But everyone's buying and selling. That's what a fair is for,' protested Stephen. He gave the other children their balloon money back and the extra penny each.

'You have to get a licence to sell things,' Brian explained. Stephen apologised and said he wouldn't do it again.

It is quite difficult to stay one jump ahead of inventive children. No sooner do you nip one activity in the bud than they think up another. Stephen finished his lunch and with eleven pence in his pocket plunged back into the fairground.

'He's had another inspiration,' said one of the others. 'He wouldn't tell us what it was.'

'I'd better follow him and make sure it's legal,' Mary said.

Mandy and I went to watch the showjumping and didn't hear what Stephen had been up to until we all assembled back at the van after the show. He had used ten of his eleven pence to hire a bucket and sponge from an impoverished pony-owning little girl, then he had spent the afternoon in the car park washing cars for 10p a time.

'Only a lick and a promise each,' he grinned, 'but with tips I made ninety pence.'

*   *   *

153

Sara and Gerry arrived at 9 p.m. and were surprised to find the place silent.

'Where is everybody?' said Sara. 'I told Gerry it would be in an uproar.'

'All the kids are asleep — we took them to a show for the whole day and they were good and ready for bed — and the minders have gone to a disco in Honiton.'

Over supper they told us all their news. The caretaking job, what their employers were like and what a lovely place they would be going to. Their duties would include maintenance of a heated swimming pool, keeping the lawns and hedges cut and painting white lines on the tennis court every weekend before the family came down from London.

'Have you got to do anything in the house apart from fighting off burglars?'

'No, they'll bring their own housekeeper cum cook with them, and a chauffeur and a nanny. We'll have more than enough to do outside. There's a kitchen garden and lots of shrubberies to see to as well as the lawns.'

'What about the dobermans — or should it be dobermen?'

'We're having them. They're going to live in heated kennels attached to the house, and we're to leave their runs open every night. Not that they're likely to get out of their comfortable beds — you've never seen such soppy dogs. The diabetic only has to have one pill a day so that's no problem.'

'And where will you be living? Is there a flat in the house?'

'We've got a cottage in the grounds, fully furnished, central heating, the lot.'

'It sounds very nice.' Brian turned to Gerry. 'What have you been doing since you left school, Gerry?'

Not a lot, it would appear. Undecided whether to be a test pilot or a brain surgeon, Gerry had let the problem lie dormant while he drifted from casual job to casual job. He wasn't a bad lad, good-looking, with a Kevin Keegan hairstyle and a relaxed friendly personality, but he was never going to set the world on fire. Brian let him steer the conversation round to fishing and rather wished he hadn't, for once Gerry was launched on his favourite topic he was hard to stop. Brian yawned.

154

He sat up though, a while later, at news of Marcus. He had been to the labour exchange and tried to get manual work as he wanted to build up his muscles after being in plaster for so long. When the clerk learned that he was an ex-civil servant he sent him to the other queue, the one for white-collar workers. Marcus protested that he'd come to sign on for manual work but neither clerk would help him.

After a few weeks of job hunting, his sickness benefit ran out and rather than take an office job he joined the staff of PGL, a big holiday centre for children in Wales.

'It must be in his genes,' we laughed. 'What's his job there?'

'I don't know,' said Sara. 'I think he was going to try for the sailing or canoeing first or failing that, just as a general dogsbody. The main thing is, it's somewhere for him to get fit again.'

The next day I took the morning off and went riding with Sara while Gerry borrowed one of Brian's rods and caught ten trout for the freezer.

'Are you sure you wouldn't like to take them home with you?' I asked. 'We don't like trout much, they don't seem to have much taste.'

'I don't like them either,' Gerry admitted. 'I spend most of my spare time catching them, then I give them away.'

'In any case we can't take trout hitch-hiking,' said Sara. 'We thought we'd drop off in Wales on the way back and go and visit Marcus.'

'When you see him would you remind him to write to us please? And ask him to tell us what they do with their holiday kids at PGL in wet weather.'

Sara and Gerry left after lunch on Wednesday and phoned up later in the evening to tell us they had arrived safely. 'Marcus says the smaller children have their own recreation room with a television, record player and dressing-up box. It doesn't sound any different from the things you do.'

The important difference as far as I could see was that we had Quentin that week and they didn't. Quentin looked upon rainy days as a challenge to his new playwriting skills and drove us and the other children potty trying to whip up some enthusiasm for rehearsals. Nobody wanted to have the playroom monopolised by Quentin's unimaginably tedious plays.

'This one's the stupidest play I've ever heard,' said seven-year-old Christopher one day.

'It's not stupid,' said Quentin.

'It *is*. You've got all the words.'

'I haven't. Fern's got some.'

'Well, two people don't make a play. You've got me down as a ballbearing. I don't want to be a ballbearing.'

Quentin snatched the script from Christopher. 'It doesn't say "ballbearing", stupid. It says "pallbearer". There's going to be a funeral and I need two people to carry the coffin.'

'I don't want a funeral,' said Suzanne. 'I'd rather have a wedding. I like weddings.'

'I haven't *written* a wedding, Suzanne, it's a funeral. I'll do you a wedding next time if you'll act in my funeral.'

'She can be a coffin carrier,' said Christopher. 'I'm not playing any more.'

'Oh please. Christopher, be a sport. You can be a "bystander clapping". I'll do some words for you in the next one if you'll act in this one.'

Christopher wanted to know why anyone was clapping at a funeral and Quentin explained.

'I'm an old man and I'm dying of old age and I get this dying wish to win a first prize at Crufts with my faithful old friend.'

'Is that Rex?'

'Yes. Rex is my Great Dane.'

'Can I be Rex?'

'*No*; Ella's going to be Rex. You're a clapping bystander. Anyway, I step forward to take the red rosette from the judge at Crufts and I say in a quavery old voice "My dear, you've made an old man very happy this day" and –'

'Why do you have to say "this day"? Why not just "today"?'

'Because that's how people talk in plays. And I step forward and drop dead. That's the dramatic bit. Then my faithful dog Rex howls as my poor old body gets carried away in a coffin. That's the end.'

'Can Hamish be a bridesmaid?' Suzanne said.

'*Yes*,' Quentin promised wildly. 'All the rabbits can be

bridesmaids if you like. Only that'll have to be the *next* play. I can't put a wedding in this one, it wouldn't go.'

He was getting overwrought, so Mary intervened at this point and suggested that anyone who wasn't in Quentin's play should join a 'pass the parcel' game that was about to start at the other end of the playroom. Quentin's entire human cast deserted him and he was left sobbing quietly into the fur of his faithful dog Rex.

'Cheer up, Quentin.' Mary was afraid Quentin's tears would start Suzanne off. 'You can work the record player if you like.'

'Will you knit me a beard, Mary?' Quentin sniffed.

'Yes all right.' Anything for a quiet life.

'Thank you.' He wiped his eyes. 'And will you knit me a bald head?'

Chapter Sixteen

'NO, YOU DAMN well *can't* have kippers for a birthday party.'

Sister Bridget wouldn't have recognised the man with a heart of gold if she could have seen Brian snarling at Hilary. It was halfway through August and all of us except Mary were beginning to show signs of wear and tear.

'I like kippers,' Hilary persisted, 'and you've got lots. He was a gloomy boy (and what boy called Hilary wouldn't be gloomy), with a horrid habit of prying into cupboards and drawers. Brian had found him investigating the contents of the freezer while the other children were having a birthday party in the playroom.

'Will you go away, Hilary, and *stop* snooping. It's none of your business what we've got in the freezer. Go on – buzz off.' Brian shut the door of the freezer room and shooed Hilary back to the party.

The gormless Hilary didn't like birthday parties. He didn't like other children and he didn't like competitive games. He and Suzanne – now in her second week and still snivelling – made a fine pair.

'I'm sick of the sight of kids,' Brian said, coming into the kitchen. Mandy and I were having a difference of opinion over the question of whether using a hoof-oil brush to glaze a pie crust would land us in court.

'Of course they won't get food poisoning Faith; I *washed* the brush before I dipped it in the milk. I'm not daft.'

We stopped arguing when Brian said he was sick of the sight of kids. This called for a united front.

'What's up, Brian?' Mandy flipped the hoof-oil brush out of sight so as not to complicate matters.

'Everything. I'm sick of finding that bloody boy creeping around like a burglar. I'm sick of never having any privacy and to crown it all, two of the piglets have got at the pansies.'

'Bracken and Briar?' I asked. Brian nodded.

Bracken and Briar were two of Rose Hip's daughters. We had become so hooked on Gloucester Old Spot pigs that we had decided to try to build up a small pure-bred herd using Rose Hip, Bracken and Briar as breeding stock. The trouble was, it was difficult on a small acreage to keep the various projects within their own allotted space. Ponies, cows and pigs could share territory without trouble, but pigs and pansies never.

'We need more land,' I said.

'We can't *afford* more land. I don't know how we're going to get through the winter as it is.'

'Gosh, that boy has got you down, hasn't he? Let's worry about next winter when it happens. We've got two more weeks of kids to get through first.'

Brian took a cup of tea and went out to the garden to grieve over the pansy casualties. Mandy and I carried the party food through to the dining room.

Prudence's ninth birthday was celebrated in traditional style. (Her mother, handing over a sealed envelope, had asked us to 'get a cake for Pru's birthday'. The envelope contained one pound – hardly enough to pay for the candles let alone the cake.) Everyone gave her a small gift and the party itself was a huge success. Julian, Anne and Mary devised a non-stop programme of games and music while Mandy and I saw to the food and vomiting. Mandy still swears it was the excitement and not the hoof-oil that caused a higher than normal regurgitation rate.

After the party Mandy and Mary went upstairs to supervise baths and bedtimes and the rest of us collapsed in the sitting room for an hour to revive before tackling the clearing up. Although all the rooms were carpeted it still sounded as though a herd of horses was cantering around overhead.

Part of the herd came downstairs again. Four crashes at the bottom of the stairs suggested that four bodies had taken the last furlong at speed. There was a firm knock at the sitting-room door.

'Come in,' said Julian. Brian and Anne looked at him with

distaste. This was against union rules. I sank down into the settee cushions and pretended to be asleep.

'It's only us,' said a cheerful voice. 'You don't have to hide.'

'Us' was the Chambers family — Clare, Joe, Dan and Ant, aged from eleven to six. Their three-year-old sister Vicky had wanted to stay for a holiday too and had been none too pleased when her parents had told her she was too young.

'We've come to say good-night,' said Clare, 'and to thank you all for giving us such a lovely day.'

Her brothers, adorable little boys with spiky French-style haircuts hugged each of us in turn and kissed us good-night. 'Thank you for the party, it was smashing.' Then they raced upstairs again.

We looked at each other, too touched to say anything for a moment.

'Did I imagine that?' said Anne. 'Did they *thank* us?'

'And kiss us?'

'Without an ulterior motive?'

It made up for all the Suzannes and Hilarys, we agreed. We had long ago given up the pretence that we didn't have favourites but Mary was the only one who was good at not letting it show.

There was another knock at the door, much quieter this time.

'They're back.'

But it was only one, Ant, the youngest.

'Hullo Ant, that was a quick night, wasn't it?' Ant bounced into the room and landed on the arm of Julian's chair.

'Mandy said I could come down again.' Ant, like all attractive and popular children, imagined that he was welcome anywhere anytime.

'Well, you can tell Mandy that we don't want you either,' said Julian, tickling Ant's bare feet. 'We're having a rest.'

'I won't stay long if you're tired,' said Ant kindly, 'but we wanted to know what we're doing tomorrow. Is it going to be sunny?'

'Dry and warm all day according to the six o'clock news,' Brian said. 'Is there anything in particular you'd like to do tomorrow?'

Ant looked at us carefully, testing the water before he jumped in. 'If you're not too tired tomorrow,' he said, with a six year old's attempt at tact, 'we'd like a sports day please. Organised races with numbers on our chests and prizes and consolation prizes for smaller people who don't win and everybody clapping and ice cubes and straws in our drinks and –'

'Yes, we've got the general gist thank you, Ant,' said Julian sagging at the thought of it all. 'Can we decide in the morning? It might be raining tomorrow.'

Bright sunshine streaming in through the bedroom window woke me early the following morning. Brian was already out in the garden working up an appetite for breakfast. I dressed and crept downstairs with my shoes in my hand. It paid to be stealthy in the morning if you didn't want to start the day umpiring, or plaiting pigtails or hunting for yesterday's shorts.

'All clear?' Mandy, another natural early riser, put her head round the kitchen door to see if it was safe to enter.

'Tea in the pot,' I whispered, nodding towards the Rayburn.

'Let's take it outside. Is there any food left over from the party?'

'Oh God, Mandy, you *couldn't*. Not at six in the morning.'

Yes she jolly well could. She heaped a plate high with cold sausage rolls and sponge cake and sat outside with me on the dew-soaked grass. Brian gave us a wave from the lower level of the garden and indicated that he woudn't mind a hand when we had finished our tea.

He was killing slugs. Slugs in Devon are about ten times the size of London ones and to kill them you have to adopt commando tactics, going in hard with the side of a trowel. What with Mandy's pre-breakfast snack and now slugs I rather wished I had stayed in bed.

'The sweetpeas need picking,' I said hopefully, but Brian insisted that de-slugging was more important. 'Mind you,' he said, 'if you've got time there's a lot of picking to do – peas, beans, courgettes and tomatoes for a start.'

He had grown so much that at times, after rain, we couldn't keep pace with the picking. Every day we took lettuces, radishes, cucumbers and tomatoes for lunch and peas or beans for supper but still it grew ahead of us. Soon it would be time to have an all-out harvesting session so that we could fill the freezers, clamp the roots and string the onions for the winter months.

The sweetpeas too were prolific. Two double rows gave us a constant supply of flowers for the house and we gave away dozens of bunches. The only things that had flopped were the pansies, our one and only cash crop. They couldn't fight wet weather, pigs and children and were so depleted we had stopped inspecting them for seed heads.

Mandy said she wouldn't mind doing a day's vegetable picking if Julian and the others would see to the children. 'Not today though, it's Anne's day off and we'll all be needed for the sports.'

After the children had had their rides they all disappeared into the playroom to 'get ready' for the afternoon sports. Mary and I were preparing lunch when the first athlete came to limber up in the kitchen. He was dressed in white shorts and plimsolls and carried the Olympic torch. This was made out of a carboard inner tube from a roll of kitchen paper and the fire coming out of the top was strips of tissue paper.

'I'm the first relay runner,' he announced running up and down on the spot. 'We're going to take turns to carry the Olympic flame after lunch.'

'Have you got orange coloured felt pen for the Olympic flame?' Mary asked.

'No, we're going to have real flames.'

Mary shot out of the kitchen faster than any athlete and returned a few minutes later with a confiscated box of matches. 'Phew, that was a near one,' she said. 'They were going to have a rehearsal with tissue paper.'

'Where did they get the matches?'

'They found them — I don't know where. If you'll finish doing the lunch I'll go and make some coloured flames.'

I set the tables, carried the food in and banged the gong. Mandy and Julian were in the top field hammering pegs into the ground to take ropes, and couldn't hear the gong so I collared the nearest small boy and sent him to tell them lunch was ready. As he turned round to leave, I caught sight of his back.

'Hey, just a minute. What have you got on your back?'

'It's my number. We thought it would be more fun to write our numbers on our skin. Those cardboard numbers you get at school always come off and you have to keep your T-shirt on for the safety-pins.'

He was number eleven. So, we saw with amazement, were thirteen of the other children.

'But *why?*' we asked. 'Why are you all number eleven?'

The answer was breathtakingly simple. Small boys are rather ribby and therefore extremely ticklish. The most painless number they could endure drawn on their bare skin was a 1 – just a few up and down strokes with a thick felt tip. And because they wanted a symmetrical look, they drew a 1 on each side of their backs, starting just under the shoulder blade and finishing at the floating rib. Any number involving a cross stroke – like a 4 – was too ticklish and nobody was skilful enough to attempt an 8 or a 5 because the ribs got in the way.

'They're all lunatics,' Julian said when he saw fourteen elevens crouched over the lunch table. 'How can I announce the winner's numbers? First number eleven, second number eleven, third number eleven. I shall go clean round the bend.'

In fact it was Anne who went round the bend first. It was her day off and as the sun was shining she had optimistically chosen to stay on the premises and sunbathe. She took a rug, book and suntan oil to a sheltered spot to drowse away the afternoon.

Her sheltered spot was fifty yards past the winning post and about as private as Piccadilly Circus in the rush hour.

'I won the sack race, Anne.'

'Look at my muscles, Anne. Anne, Anne, wake *up*. Do you think I'll win the long jump?'

She felt too sleepy to make the effort to move out of the sports field and put up with the competitors in the sack, egg and spoon and potato races, but when the losers of the apple bobbing contest showered her with icy water and complained that something or other 'wasn't fair' she gathered up her rug and fled.

163

Brian came out of the vegetable garden for a break and sat on the grass to watch the last few events.

'Don't sit there, Brian — you're in goal,' Mandy warned.

'Goal?'

'Football dribbling. They've got to shoot between those two buckets when they've dribbled twenty yards.'

Brian moved to the sidelines. 'Have you switched the electric fence off?' he asked. 'If you're going to have footballs flying around some of them are bound to go into the pigs' area.'

'I switched it off before we started,' said Mandy. 'Look it's quite dead.' She bent down and grasped the single strand electric wire.

'*Shit*! What *cretin* switched the fence on? Go on, own up. Whoever did it is going to get a bucket of water over their heads.'

The children, who were all convulsed with laughter, debated whether to unmask the culprit and have the fun of seeing the punishment carried out, or to keep quiet and hope that the grown-ups would make further fools of themselves. They kept quiet. 'I've got telepathic powers.' Mandy glared at them. 'I know who did it.'

'If you know who did it why did you put your hand on the wire, Mandy?' someone asked.

'Come on, lets get on with the next game,' said one of the boys who had a four point lead. The overall winner was going to get a box of Maltesers.

Julian and Mary umpired the next game which involved two relay teams shooting as many goals as possible in ten minutes. All went well until Elizabeth the cow appeared and ambled towards the pile of footballs.

'Who let Elizabeth out of the yard?' said Brian.

'The same person who switched the fence on I expect,' I said. 'Oh look everybody — look at Elizabeth.'

Elizabeth sniffed the footballs suspiciously then lowered her head and poked one of her horns right through one of the balls. It deflated with a hiss and Elizabeth tossed her head in alarm and set off up the field at a gallop with the football impaled on her horn.

The commotion woke some of the piglets who had been dozing in the sun and they scattered to let Elizabeth through. The broken football fell off her head and the little pigs squealed with pleasure and started to tear their new toy to bits.

'I'd better take it away from them in case they swallow any,' Mandy laughed. The piglets followed her back to the Olympic arena and with joyful little snorts trotted straight into the pile of footballs which Julian had stacked ready for the game. There were footballs, piglets and children everywhere and a party of holiday-makers strolling along the road at the top of the paddock parked their rucksacks and whisked out cameras.

'It's a traditional Devon fertility dance,' Brian called out to them. 'Makes the crops grow.' They laughed so much their photographs must have come out rather fuzzily. We imagined them showing their friends the holiday snapshots and wondering why a group of children were all numbered eleven.

Julian collected the scattered footballs and consulted his programme. 'We'll go straight on with the next game,' he said. 'Football's off.'

Brian, who had recently attended a Smallholders' Association lecture on Grassland Management watched some more races with mixed feelings. The children were having the time of their lives, but plainly sports days did not play a very useful part in the management of a mixed ley.

'I don't want to do this next year.'

'What, sports days?' I said, being deliberately obtuse.

'You know perfectly well what I mean. I don't want to do children's holidays any more.'

'Nor do I,' I agreed.

He looked at me in astonishment. 'I thought you *enjoyed* it.'

'I did. I still do a lot of the time. But it's tremendously hard work, cooking six hundred and two meals a week —'

'You can't count lunches.'

'Don't split hairs. Six hundred and two meals counting lunches and I'm tired of it. Even a trained chef would be tired of it and cooking's not my thing.'

'You're not as bad as you used to be.' Some men have the knack of paying compliments. 'And we've got to do something about the overdraft.'

One way to lessen the impact of a letter from the bank is to admire the skilful way they avoid the use of the word *money*. The latest letter respectfully reminded Brian that he would shortly be exceeding his 'facility'. Quite good. Not as good as one which referred to 'your twelve month projected budget proposal' but a game effort nonetheless.

'There must be other ways of making a living,' I said. 'How about a model farm open to the public just in the daytime? No dinners. No breakfasts.' Even as I said it, I realised that with no overnight guests there wouldn't be any need for such a large house. That would be a wrench. On the other hand, less house could equal more land. Land that would not have its delicate structure (The Soil Course, Part One) disturbed by forty plim-solled feet . . .

But the middle of a paddock temporarily turned into a sports arena is not one of the best places in which to plan a new career and we had to break off as Suzanne burst into tears because nobody would partner her for the three-legged race and several other children plonked their hefty legs in our laps to be shackled up.

'I don't think you should use binder twine to tie round your ankles,' Brian told one of them. 'Look, you've got grooves in your skin where it's too tight. Haven't you got a handker-chief?'

'Yes, but I've used it to clean cow muck off my socks.'

'You're not wearing socks.'

'I took them off, they went all green with cow muck. Why is cow muck green, Brian?'

'Because cows eat grass.'

'Horses eat grass but theirs is brown. And we eat raspberries and jelly and ours is —'

'Is that tight enough?' Brian said hastily, knotting the cord.

'Yes thank you, but actually you've tied me to the wrong leg. Dan's my partner.'

Brian threw me a despairing look so I took the pile of legs from him. He returned to his gardening and was spared the scene where a wailing Suzanne brought off the amazing feat of failing to win the three-legged race even though she ran with-out the handicap of a partner.

166

The obstacle race was the grand finale. The children had to crawl under, over and through various hazards, throw a ball at a target and jump in a sack for the last twenty yards. One snake-hipped small boy dived into a hessian tunnel with such vigour that his trousers came off *en route* and he emerged at the other end wearing only an embarrassed grin.

Dan was the overall winner and handed round his Maltesers until they were all gone. In return he demanded a bite out of everyone else's consolation prize — a bar of chocolate — which led to some heated talk about fractions. Most of the children hadn't 'got up to fractions' yet.

'I can do division,' someone boasted. The others were impressed.

'And I can multiply by ten.'

'So can I. You just put a nought on.'

'Where?'

'At the end, pea-brain.'

'Pea-brain yourself, clever dick. If you put a *vest* on you, you put it on at the beginning, don't you? How do you know noughts go on at the end?'

Chapter Seventeen

LETTERS FROM Sara ceased once she and Gerry moved to their caretaking job and had the use of a phone as part of their wages. For two green youngsters they seemed to be coping remarkably well with the estate. They had a ride-on mower for the parkland grass and formal lawns, a flymo for the rough edges, and a tractor-drawn cutter for maintaining the grassy rides through some woodland.

There were a few mishaps of course, mainly in the greenhouses. They drowned some things, roasted others, and sent the occasional casualty to Brian for a post-mortem report. In the formal rose garden they wielded secateurs with such enthusiasm that the roses cringed back to their briar stocks (we hated standard roses anyway, said Sara defensively) and the hydrangea petiolaris, which was supposed to clamber prettily up the walls of the house, tried to make a run for it across the lawn. Secateur-happy Sara chopped four-foot tendrils off the parent plants *before* phoning Brian for pruning instructions.

'You vandal,' he said. 'What do you think they are, bonsais? You train them — no pruning.'

'Oh. Will they grow again?'

'Probably, if they don't die of shock. Are you giving the beds plenty of water?'

'I think so. It's quite hard to know what plenty means. We gave the greenhouse tomatoes plenty and they split.'

Patiently Brian delivered a short lecture on greenhouse cultivation, and recommended some gardening books. He quite enjoyed these gardening by-proxy sessions; it's a rare thing for a parent to be actually consulted by a teenage daughter.

In our turn we sought advice. How were we to earn a living from seven acres if we really did give up doing children's holidays?

'You can't,' said our new SHA friends and acquaintances. 'Not unless you go intensive and you know what *that* means.'

We did in theory. But was it true? Could factory farming be as bad as our reading led us to believe?

Yes, and yes again. On the principle of 'don't knock it until you've tried it' we booked appointments to visit two intensive units.

The first place we saw was a piggery. Two hundred sows were housed in a long shed with a concrete floor sloping to a dung channel which ran down the middle. On either side of the channel were one hundred pens, each about three feet wide and one pig length long. The sows were tied to the sides of the pens by chains linked to leather harnesses round their bodies.

They were virtually immobilised, being unable to turn round, scratch, or lie on their sides. Through some metal bars in front of each one of them there was a water bowl and a feeding trough. Beyond that was a blank wall.

They spent their entire lives chained up like prisoners in a medieval dungeon. They were artificially inseminated *in situ* and farrowed in another shed with a different arrangment – called a farrowing crate – to restrict them. For any creature, to be deprived of exercise, daylight and companionship is appalling. For pigs, highly intelligent, sensitive animals as they are, it is utterly barbaric.

The shed was well ventilated with louvred slits in the roof, and the dung channel was scrubbed and clean. It was some while before it dawned on us that the putrid smell pervading the shed was coming from the sows themselves – from their sour breath, unhealthy pale skin and open sores where the leather harnesses had rubbed.

The man who owned this hell – he called himself a farmer – trotted out the usual defence platitude that unhappy animals won't breed. The fact that he was able to look without shame or pity on the chained pigs precluded any chance of civilised argument so we left.

He was not breaking any law. Forcing animals to gaze at a brick wall for four or five years is perfectly legal.

The next visit was to a veal unit. Here, living conditions were a lot better than those at the piggery. Calves from a few hours old were housed individually in wooden crates. They had room to turn and lie down. There was fresh straw to lie on and free access to a water bowl. Their stockman bucket-fed them twice a day. All they lacked was a mother, other company, a balanced diet (veal calves are kept short of iron so that the meat is pale), fresh air and an MP to defend them.

Oh well, back to the drawing board. We sent letters of support to animal welfare groups and letters of complaint to Westminster then turned again to the thorny problem of how to earn a living.

Meanwhile, parents were booking children in for the following year. This was tricky : should we tell everybody we were closing? We might regret it if no workable alternative had suggested itself by next year. So for the time being we did nothing.

The last ten days of the school holidays took priority in any case and we eased our consciences by giving the children outing after outing. We went to Bicton Horse Show, Dunster Agricultural Show, Honiton's Steam Engine rally, two small village fêtes and a goat show. And, as a last fling, to a fairground.

In the interests of safety, it had to be an 'all hands to the pump' outing with tight supervision. Each of us chose three or four children and stuck close to them throughout a seemingly endless evening. If our charges wanted to go on the Sky Diver or the Big Wheel, there we would be, clutching them for support – our support – as we whirled and plunged and rocketed through the air.

It seemed hard to believe that we were *paying* to leave our stomachs three hundred feet above a seaside town. 'Fantastic,' they screamed. 'Magic! Let's go round again.' And again and again and again.

Mandy displayed the sort of courage that I thought only kamikaze pilots possessed. With my own eyes I saw her eat three fried doughnuts and a plate of winkles before embarking on a couple of trips in a Whirly Rocket. She stepped off afterwards as fresh as a daisy. Not so the rest of us.

The children were very sweet and fussed over us with touching concern. They agreed that they had been rather selfish in expecting us to keep having goes on the Big Dipper and they had a whip round to treat us to a tombola ticket each.

When at last all the pocket money had been spent they helped us back to the minibus and offered to count themselves in. 'You're tired,' they said. 'We can do it to save you the trouble.'

'I'll count them in,' Brian said, handing me the keys. 'You drive, then I can sit in the back and die until we get home.' His face, after several Big Wheel sessions, looked like a dropped omelet.

The minders piled into Mary's car and set off before us. I started the engine and swung the bus across the fairground car park and on to the main road. We settled down to a steady 40 mph and watched the tail lights of Mary's car disappearing into the distance.

'ROLL ov-er, ROLL ov-er,' the children sang. 'And they all rolled over and one fell out and the little one said ROLL ov-er ROLL ov-er and then there were only nine in the bed and . . .'

The engine purred smoothly. Funny the way engines go better at night, I thought, and hasn't the old bus done us proud since it was serviced. Never a hiccup now and even the heater works. Perhaps we might sell it once the children have gone and get something smaller, a pick-up truck maybe, or an estate so we can carry animals in the back. . .

That did it of course. Ford Transit minibus gremlins are as touchy as prima donnas. They have several spiteful ways of retaliating and on this occasion it was a puncture. The bus bumped along on five of its six wheels and I pulled in at the next layby.

'Wake up,' I said to Brian. 'We've got a puncture.' Brian's reply was unprintable. The children nudged each other and giggled. 'Can we help?' they said.

'It would help if you'd all stay in your seats while Brian jacks the bus up.'

'Isn't it dark? Can we have the lights on?'

'No, we'd better save the battery.' Brian and I climbed out and struck matches to see what needed doing. The front offside tyre was as flat as a cow pat.

It took half an hour and a whole box of Swan Vestas — we

had forgotten the torch – to fit the spare tyre. The job would have been easier if it had been safe to get the children out before jacking up but the A38 is no place to start losing children in the dark.

And so – in a layby kneeling on the road groping for wheel nuts in a greasy hub cap – ended the last day of holidays for unaccompanied children. The kids sang 'Over the Hills and Far Away' which was a welcome change from 'ROLL ov-er' and asked us if we knew that hub caps make smashing frisbies.

'Where have you been?' exclaimed the others when we got back. We told them about the puncture and hurried off to bath before the children invaded the bathrooms.

In the morning Brian had recovered enough to seduce one of the mothers on platform 1 at Taunton station. Well, it started on platform 1 and was consummated, to my fury, in Taunton's poshest teashop where they serve huge slices of gooey gâteau and real coffee. He can seduce away to his heart's content, but I felt it was rubbing my nose in it to tell me that the Other Woman had had éclairs with her coffee. Two éclairs.

'The ones that squish the cream out sideways when you bite them?' I asked masochistically. He claimed not to have noticed and this I could well believe. Alan's mother was very attractive if you like women with flawless skins, shapely figures and Gucci shoes.

'I told her we're stopping the children's holidays,' he said. 'She was very sorry, she wanted Alan to come again.'

'Tough,' I muttered. Two éclairs. 'And tough on Alan.'

'I'll buy you a pig if you like,' he offered. I weakened. How could anyone resist such an olive branch?

'Two pigs?' Brian always overbid his hand.

'Done,' I said.

Within minutes of the last car departing we were in the vegetable garden planning a harvesting campaign. It was good to have an urgent job to do just now because without the kids things felt a bit flat. The minders too had gone. Julian and Anne back to university, Mary to her London primary school and Mandy to her parents and horses. She would be dropping in from time to time to give us a hand but for the present there was just us and an acre of crops. All through the season we had picked enough to meet daily demands but now, with two 13c.ft. freezers emptied for the occasion, it was time to think big.

Neither of us had had any experience of freezing vegetables – the previous year's drought had killed off most of the crops and before that we hadn't owned a freezer – so we decided to be on the safe side and blanch everything.

Luckily before we both had nervous breakdowns – imagine blanching 200 lb of runner beans using normal household equipment – an SHA member called Jayne came to the rescue. Jayne was a Cordon Bleu-trained chef who ran a mixed small-holding in Somerset.

'Blanch beans,' she exclaimed in answer to my telephoned SOS. 'Good heavens, who has time to go by the book in September?'

'They say in my cookery book you must blanch everything or it goes on decomposing in the freezer.'

'Well, they would, wouldn't they? I mean people who write cookery books have got to cover themselves. And I don't suppose for a moment that whoever wrote that was actually growing the stuff. I've been freezing for years and you can take my word that beans, peas, tomatoes and sweetcorn are fine if you put them straight in the freezer directly you've picked them. If you've got time, it's better to puree the tomatoes because that takes up less room, but if not, just chuck them in whole. They come out like billiard balls. How's Elizabeth?' Jayne was inordinately fond of Jersey cows and was building up a small pedigree milking herd.

'Fine. She's going to a bull next heat.'

'Jersey?'

'No, a friend's Hereford.'

'Is she still milking well?'

'Over four gallons a day. The holiday children have gone so we're getting two more pigs to mop up the surplus milk.'

I returned to the harvest with renewed enthusiasm. For me the best bit of the gardening cycle is picking the crop – Brian prefers planting – and it had been very frustrating to have a bottleneck of vegetables building up in the kitchen waiting to

173

be blanched. For the rest of the growing season we picked ten to fifteen pounds of beans a day, runners and French, and froze them within minutes of picking.

There was a longish spell of settled weather at this time and the tomatoes ripened quickly. We picked a few pounds each day and followed Jayne's instructions, dropping them into polythene bags which we then lowered carefully into the freezer. Overnight they became as hard as marbles and could then be crammed into every vacant nook in the second freezer, the cornucopia.

The potatoes we clamped, using a technique which looked complicated in the gardening book illustrations, but which turned out to be so easy and so enjoyable that we actually spent as much time admiring and photographing each stage as doing the work.

First we dug up the potatoes and threw the spent haulm to one side for later composting. The potatoes were laid out in rows for twenty-four hours and turned occasionally to dry off evenly. Then we heaped them on to a bed of dry straw and built up a pyramid of alternating layers — straw, spuds, straw — finishing off with a topping of dry earth. Then we shovelled earth up the four sides of the pyramid leaving an air vent on each side so that the potatoes could sweat. We estimated that there were about five hundredweight in the clamp, enough to last us for a year and leave some for bartering.

There are those who bore their friends with holiday snap-shots or ciné films of their cousin's wedding. We are vegetable bores. We have pictures of parsnips in rows and in close up, swedes, turnips, beetroots, carrots ditto; fine Ailsa Craigs before and after stringing; pumpkins, courgettes, tomatoes and sweetcorn caught at all stages from two-leafed infants to impressive maturity.

At the drop of a hat we will set up our projector and screen, lock the door and subject any casual dropper-in to *hours* of vegetable transparencies. It's such fun growing things, and in the long winter evenings, such pleasure to get out the pictures and recall the smell of freshly turned earth and the feel of the sun on your back as you drive the fork under a clump of carrots. Our dearest and most long suffering friends, Anne and

174

Geoffrey, who are both townies to the marrow, once ended a letter: 'and looking forward to seeing you on January 2nd even if it does mean we shall have to endure your endless turnip transparencies.'

Nipping out for a bit of social life during September became a busman's holiday. Every single one of our new smallholding friends was digging and clamping, picking, freezing and bottling. There was a wonderful feeling of camaraderie as the group prepared to batten down the hatches for winter. Betty's barter board groaned with postcards – runners for pork, runners for cream, runners for trout. Devon seemed to be sinking under the weight of runner beans after a wettish summer.

Labour was in short supply though. There were many postcards plaintively asking for muscle in exchange for asparagus, venison, trout or beef. People with sturdy sons to lend out were going to be able to eat in style this winter.

Some of the notices spoke volumes in a couple of words: 'Unplucked poultry' was plainly being offered by someone so bogged down by their vegetable glut that they hadn't had time to do more than kill the birds. A 'virile but frustrated Buff Orpington' needed a new home because his incestuous habits were endangering the flock, genetically speaking that is.

One of our favourites was 'Damaged chain-link fencing' which looked innocent enough until you noticed that another part of the board on another postcard the same advertiser wanted to be rid of 'Five in-lamb ewes, very agile'. A case of throwing in the sponge obviously. 'Castrations for cream' was intriguing. How many testicles we wondered, would equal a pint of cream? (Impoverished cream cravers might like to know that the answer is six.)

Money was hardly ever resorted to as a means of exchange in the early days of the SHA. We were all broke, even those who went out to work, and finances were discussed with a frankness that is maybe only possible between people whose incomes are below taxable level.

Everyone but the lunatic fringe in the group agreed that their holdings would never earn them a living. If they did they would be farmers and into a whole new ball game. The dozen or so friends that Brian and I made within the association had other means: some taught, some sold their craftwork, others their services.

Throughout the busy autumn we racked our brains. How could we two townies with no skills and a combined IQ of about fifty earn a living on seven acres?'

'More pansies?' I suggested, and ducked as Brian turned the hose on me. The cheque for our harvested pansy seed was framed and pinned on the kitchen wall: 'Pay Brian Addis' it said on the top line. So far so good: 'seventy pence only.'

The word 'only' seemed to us both unnecessary and a trifle cruel.

Chapter Eighteen

MANDY WAS A great help during the autumn months. She had time on her hands while she waited for an apprenticeship vacancy in a yard of her parents' choice, and would often drop in to give us a hand during the day. She had three horses of her own to see to at home, a mare with a suckling foal and two unbroken colts. As none of these took up much time, she started a manure round, bagging up droppings and straw in the mornings and delivering it to muck-starved gardeners in the evenings when her father was free, albeit reluctantly, to act as chauffeur.

'You always seem to be able to think up ways of earning money,' I said to her one day. 'What would you do if you had this place and no capital?'

'Give riding lessons of course. You've got five ponies eating their heads off when they could be earning you two pounds an hour.'

'Me? Give riding lessons? I'm not qualified.'

'No, but you're old.'

'*Old*?' I said touchily. 'And since when has thirty-nine been old?'

'Keep your hair on. What I mean is, you'd get a riding licence without being qualified if the council inspector thinks you've had enough years of experience. You'd better say you're fifty, not thirty-nine on the application form and wear something dead boring like crimplene slacks when they come to see you.'

'How about incontinence pads and a walking frame?' I suggested. We developed this theme until our sides ached then went to find Brian to see what he thought of the new scheme. He was all for anything that might bring in some money so I sent off to the local council for an application form. Meanwhile, Mandy coached us both on the questions the inspector would ask.

I drew the line at putting my age down as fifty and compromised at an elderly forty-five. (Sara, of course, was in stitches when I phoned her and told her that I too had lied about my age in order to get a job.) The rest of the questions on the form I answered truthfully. I could offer light hacking and elementary instruction. I did not have an indoor ménage, a cross-country course, livery facilities or a polo string. Yes, I did have separate toilet facilities clients for the use of. No, I did not have TB, epilepsy, VD or defective vision. Just a defective bank balance.

The inspector called. Inspectors love drains, Mandy had said, so we were all prepared with rods and white paint. Brian is rather keen on drains himself and co-operated willingly in the Drains Test, which involved pouring white water down holes and being surprised when it reappeared at the outlet pipes.

'Superb drainage,' said the inspector, Brian glowed with pride and offered him a cigarette.

'No Smoking,' said the inspector, in capital letters. 'You'll have to put up a No Smoking notice in the stables.' Brian stuffed his Players back in his hip pocket and suffered withdrawal symptoms until the inspector had gone.

'Do you want to see their teeth now?' I asked.

'Whose teeth?' said the inspector.

'Mine, if you like, ha ha.'

No, he didn't want to look at my teeth (I'll *sue* Boots Anti-Wrinkle Cream) nor the horses'. Teeth and feet came under Veterinary Examination, which was a different department. He was concerned only with drains, exits and entrances and, unbelievably, the distance between the manure heap and the General Public.

The next stage of the proceedings would be the inspector's written report on the suitability or otherwise of our buildings. If all was well we would then be inspected by the Fire Department and the Vet's Department. As to the question of my having no formal qualification to teach, that was perfectly all right, Madam, your age and experience are sufficient to satisfy

178

the Department that you are a responsible applicant. (Good old Mandy.)

The responsible applicant was too impatient to wait for the council to get cracking on the other inspections, and put an advertisement in a local paper offering light hacking and elementary instruction on quiet ponies.

The first person who phoned in answer to the ad was a man with a lovely Richard Burton voice. His firm had sent him to Devon on a three-month engineering project and he wanted to take the opportunity to learn to ride while he was living in such beautiful countryside. We were getting on like a house on fire until he told me he was six foot two and weighed twelve and a half stone. I had to tell him that although he sounded right up my street, my ponies would write to their union if they were asked to carry more than ten stone. I gave him the phone number of a riding school (Tony's) where he would be well looked after, and with mutual regret we rang off. (In later weeks I learned through Tony that I hadn't missed much. Golden Voice had a barrel chest and a face like – quote – a rat's arsehole.)

But I got three other customers, small girls with conventional faces and no weight problems. Two of them booked Saturday morning rides and the other, Sunday afternoons. The rides were supposed to last one hour, but remembering my own agonies as a ten-year-old when the weekly hour was nearly up, I didn't trouble to clock watch. It was nice taking them on a one to one basis, rambling along the lanes and cantering round the edges of a farmer friend's fields.

All three firmly ordered their parents to collect them 'as late as possible' so that they could spend time with the ponies after riding. They tidied the tack room, filled hay nets and inhaled the bouquet coming off the manure heap with a fine disregard for the health inspector's notion about manure heaps and the General Public.

The spell of fine weather ended and for some unaccountable reason the rain brought with it raiding parties of pigeons and rabbits. They came at dusk as if they knew the dogs would be stretched contentedly in front of the fire and wouldn't disturb them. The pigeons nipped away at the precious broccoli buds, leaving the young sprouts for the rabbits.

It got so bad that Brian borrowed Ursula's shotgun and started a counter attack. The first casualty was a fat pigeon which thudded to the ground with such force it sent up a spray of water from the mud.

'Good shot, Brian, what a whopper,' I shouted, darting out to retrieve it. 'That'll teach it to pinch our broccoli.'

But unhappily it was not a broccoli pincher at all. It was a racing pigeon with a metal ring on its leg and a crop full of its owner's grain.

'Oh crumbs.' I stroked the blue plumage and admired its bulging muscles. 'Why did you have to shoot that one in particular?'

'What the hell do you expect me to do — get their names and addresses before I shoot them? I just aimed at the biggest.'

The bang from the gun frightened off all the other pigeons so we never knew if the dead one was part of a racing group or an odd one that had strayed off course. Shooting didn't seem a very effective way of getting rid of pigeons anyway, it was such a bore having to wait for them to regroup after a shot. And it was never on for rabbits, what with cats lurking beneath hedges and the cow always getting in the way just as Brian was about to pull the trigger. Anything Brian did was all right by Elizabeth; he could have turned a machine gun on her and she would have licked his face.

One day I was in Taunton market keeping my finger on the pulse of pig prices when I got talking to a girl called Liz, thirtyish, blonde and energetic. It was a case of instant friendship. The conversation turned to rabbit control and Liz said: 'Ferrets, that's your answer.'

Liz was keen on ferrets and with good reason. When she and her husband Graham had met each other they were both miserably married to other people and it was a bit tricky starting their affair without the respective spouses getting suspicious. So Graham bought Liz a ferret and they started meeting in the long summer evenings, ostensibly to catch rabbits but actually to do what any red-blooded couple do in a poppy-strewn cornfield when the sun is setting.

I found this story rather romantic, but Brian thought it was disgusting. 'How can you cuddle a girl smelling of *ferrets*?' he said.

'Well, it's like garlic. If you both smell the same you don't notice.'

'Tell me again from the beginning. You met this girl Liz at Taunton market and she immediately gave you a blow by blow account of her sex life? Why can't things like that happen to me?'

'I wish you'd shut up and listen for five minutes instead of being facetious. Liz and Graham are coming to supper tonight.'

'And I suppose they're bringing their ferrets,' he said sarcastically.

'Yes.'

'Oh, *no*. You've gone too far this time. I am *not* having ferrets to supper. I shall go to —'

'Do you want sprouts?' I interrupted.

'I don't want anything. I'm going out.'

'Do you want sprouts? Sprouts in the garden I mean? Liz and Graham are giving up a whole evening to come here and help us to get rid of the rabbits that are eating *your* sprouts. They're bringing ferrets, a dog, and a gun. I think it's called lamping.' I waited for him to say 'Who the dog, or the gun?', but surprisingly he didn't, so I continued: 'And after we've caught all the rabbits we'll come indoors and have some supper. The ferrets can stay outside in their Land Rover.'

'Promise?' he said warily. 'You're not going to say "Ah, poor ferrets," and bring them into the sitting room, are you?'

'Promise.'

'I still don't understand how a complete stranger came to be telling you about romps in a poppy field after five minutes' acquaintance. How did the conversation start — hullo, my name's Liz and I get turned on by ferrets?'

'More or less. We were leaning on the rails looking at weaners and we got talking about the weather and the harvest — Graham's head tractor chap on a huge farm — and that led to rabbits. I said we didn't know how to control them, and Liz told me how she got interested in ferreting. So I invited them here to have a go at ours.'

They arrived just before dark and we all had a quick cup of coffee before getting down to business. The rain was coming down in a steady drizzle and Brian was not exactly eager to don boots and go outside.

'Shall we postpone it for another evening?' he suggested. The log fire did look inviting. We persuaded him that unchewed sprouts were worth getting pneumonia for and propelled him out.

Graham and Liz had brought an experienced ferret called Doris and a springer spaniel called Trudi. She was liver and white, scarcely more than a puppy, and so exuberant she had to stay on the lead to start with. We walked across the fields to a hedge whose banks were full of rabbit holes and Graham fixed some green nets over several sections where he thought the rabbits would bolt.

'I'll slip Doris down the burrow at this end,' he explained, 'and she'll frighten them out into the nets.' He groped deep into his coat pocket and pulled out a reluctant looking Doris. She took one look at the freezing rain and tried to wriggle up Graham's warm sleeve. Brian suddenly decided that he liked ferrets after all and said he didn't know they were so intelligent.

'Wake up, Doris.' Liz tickled Doris under her tiny chin and Doris yawned, showing two rows of razor-sharp teeth.

'Do you ever get bitten?' I asked.

'No, not by Doris.' Her sister Gladys can be a bit of a grump, but Doris is a friendly old thing.'

The rabbits must have found Doris friendly too for not one bolted. We waited outside the burrows for over half an hour, our fingers and toes getting steadily more numb. Trudi the spaniel tugged at her lead and whined with impatience while Graham made encouraging noises down the rabbit holes.

'Who's a clever girl Doris, send 'em out, good girl.'

Doris slithered down into the maze and found herself a cozy spot to settle. We could picture her swapping knitting patterns and recipes with her new mates down there and tutting over the strange ways of humans who expect you to turn out on a night not fit for a dog.

'I can't understand it,' said Graham. 'She's a great little

worker as a rule.' He went back to the Land Rover for a torch and shone it down all the holes in turn.

'Doris, Dor-is,' he called. 'Come out now, there's a good girl.'

Eventually he found her, curled up in a ball on a cushion of moss. 'She's asleep,' he said crossly, and got his arm all muddy reaching down the hole to retrieve her.

'What next?' I asked.

'Supper?' said Brian.

'Lamping,' said Liz. 'Trudi's getting cold.'

'*Trudi's* getting cold,' Brian moaned, and watched enviously as Doris was put in a hay-lined box in the back of the Land Rover.

We are still not quite sure what lamping is. It seemed to be a wet walk round the edge of the field punctuated by outbreaks of swearing as vicious brambles scored cuts across our faces.

'This'll do,' said Graham, and stopped. It was pitch dark by now, and we cannoned into him. Trudi got her paw trodden on and told the world that every bone in her body was broken. Brian said conversationally wasn't lamping fun, and how did couples without ferrets or lamps manage to keep their relationships stimulating?

All four of us collapsed with laughter. Liz pulled herself together first and switched on the lamp, a huge battery powered contraption that weighed a ton and sent out a beam like a searchlight.

'The rabbits get mesmerised by the light and can't move,' she whispered.

We stood quietly for ten minutes or so watching the needles of rain driving through the yellow shaft of light. Trudi whined.

'I think I can see a rabbit,' said Liz.

'It's got swimming trunks on,' Brian muttered. Trudi saw the rabbit and bounded towards it as Graham raised his gun.

'*Down* Trudi!' Graham roared. The shot went harmlessly into the bank.

'Sodding dog.' Graham reloaded and Liz made Trudi sit at heel while she cast the lamp light to and fro across the field.

'Right, let's try again,' said Graham. 'Send her in Liz.'

Trudi was sent into the undergrowth to flush out more rabbits. Once again Liz caught a rabbit in the light and again Trudi spoiled Graham's shot by getting in the firing line. By nine-thirty we were all soaked to the skin and every rabbit in Devon was tittering behind its paw.

Back in the house the unrepentant Trudi shook herself vigorously and hogged the fire much to old Honey's annoyance. Honey got up stiffly and withdrew to her basket to sulk. Liz and I towelled Trudi dry and left her to steam in front of the fire with Ella and Parsley for company.

After some piping hot spaghetti bolognese and a few glasses of red wine which a grateful parent had left we were able to see the funny side of the rabbitless evening. I remembered a letter I had read in *Farmers' Weekly* by a man who scattered lions' dung round the edges of his garden because, he claimed, the smell deterred rabbits for miles around.

'I don't mean we should *keep* lions,' I said, when the others had stopped wetting themselves. 'But how about hiring a lorry and buying a load of manure from a zoo?' Brian, who was in high spirits now that he wasn't standing out in the rain, said that if I started flinging lions' dung around the garden, he would go back to his mum and keep in touch by postcard.

We all had a lot in common. Liz and Graham were looking for ways to earn a living too; they lived in a tied cottage which went with Graham's job and were not happy with the arrangement. Graham worked long hours at a job which carried a lot of responsibility and not much money, and Liz stayed at home looking after their four children — three of hers and one of his — and tending their few acres. They wanted a place of their own where they could keep more livestock and maybe start a small business.

By the time the third bottle was empty the four of us had solved each other's problems and even a few global ones. Liz and I would run a riding school cum animal sanctuary, Graham would have his own farm and Brian would do experimental research on plant breeding and be Prime Minister in his spare time.

It was 1 a.m. before they left. 'You must come in good weather next time,' we said, stepping out into the teeming rain. 'The view is sensational on a sunny day.'

Liz, with Mandy-like common sense said: 'But you can't eat the view, can you?'

Chapter Nineteen

THE SMALLHOLDERS' Association Autumn Social was going to be a barn dance, it was decided in committee. One of our members had buildings that were just right, with an upstairs barn for the dancers and plenty of space below to set out trestle tables and straw bale seating for a hundred or so.

Normally I avoid parties. Having a husband who can dance like Fred Astaire is off-putting for someone who has to provide shin guards for unwary partners; and other party rituals like where-do-you-live, and isn't-rush-hour-traffic-ghastly, leave me glancing furtively at my watch and wishing I was in bed with book and cocoa.

But the SHA socials were events to be looked forward to for weeks ahead. It gave you a good warm feeling to 'belong' and to develop friendships with people who shared a love of the land, warts and all.

We took Mandy to the barn dance. She looked a knockout in figure-hugging pants made of velvet, and a frilly shirt top, and was soon whisked away for a dance by someone's teenage son. Brian and I spotted a group of our friends at the bar. We waved and started to pick our way round the trestle tables to join them.

The barn was temporarily lit by, of all things, a candelabra, which a resourceful do-it-yourselfer had rigged up for the evening, so there was no excuse for what happened next. Brian, not looking where he was going, took a step forward and found to his disgust that he had put his leg halfway down a full slurry pit. The boards covering the pit were wobbly and his foot had slipped.

'Pooh, yuck,' said our friends at the bar.

'Keep your distance.'

'Was that a new dance step, Brian?'

'He's auditioning for Dyno-Rod.'

'Or Oklahoma. When-I-take-you-out-of-the-slurry. . .'

'Very funny,' said Brian. 'Ha ha. Buy me a beer and I'll do it again.' He went to find a tap outside, but even after he had washed the worst off he continued to pong. The report of the barn dance which appeared in the next SHA newsletter (an earnest monthly bulletin full of technical tips and write-ups of lectures and demonstrations but most eagerly read for its page of 'For Sale' and 'Wanted' items) said that he added a certain flavour to the already warm atmosphere.

But what's a whiff of slurry among friends? It certainly went with the conversations. Someone started the ball rolling with retained afterbirths, and in no time everybody was deep in debate: where can I hire a Suffolk tup; hedges as a crop; coppic-ing; is half a pig profitable; pea-eating mice; pregnancy test-ing; abbatoirs, shall we have an abbatoir outing; so and so's got some bee-keeping equipment for sale − he's giving up after all those stings.

From cabbages to King Edwards the conversation flowed. The enquiry 'How are you?' took on a deeper meaning when smallholders said it because they asked after specific bits of each other − Hi Rob, how's your back? Betty dear, haven't seen you for ages. Is your hip better? That's a nasty bruise, Penny. Have you tried him in a standing martingale?

Comparisons of osteopaths were popular among people whose life styles led to all sorts of physical breakdowns. Like the old bangers most of us drove, our bodies were always in need of servicing − a torn cartilage here, a displaced disc or two (or even three in the haymaking season) there. Not many of us could spare the time to be mended by GPs whose 'pain killers and bed rest' prescriptions were quite unrealistic for patients who had farm animals to look after. So osteopaths were much sought after, and if you found a good one who could fix you in a couple of sessions and who didn't charge the earth you shared him with your fellows.

We swapped vet stories too but vets didn't play a very large part in our lives. This may sound paradoxical for smallholders but the fact was, we nearly all took the greatest pride in caring for our animals properly and would have thought it shameful to let them fall ill. Obviously there were accidents, and a vet would be called to stitch lacerated tissue, but speaking generally we depended on vets for prophylaxis.

Halfway through the evening the pounding feet of the dancers overhead stopped and the accordion wheezed a last note.

'Feeding time. Gosh, I'm ravenous.' Mandy joined us at the bar and Brian bought her a lager. She was scarlet from her exertions and looked like a scrum-half on a rainy day at Twickenham.

'Been doing handstands up there?'

'No need to be sarky, Brian, it's as dusty as anything, that floor. It looks like a grain store. Why didn't you come and dance?'

'Not our scene thanks,' I said. 'Besides, Brian's got his own method of looking like something the cat dragged in.'

'What is it?' said Mandy, bending down to look at his green trouser leg. 'It looks like slurry – cripes, it *is* slurry. Can't you keep away from manure, Brian, just for a few hours?'

'Go and currycomb your face, young Mandy, and don't be cheeky.'

Mandy went to have a wash. We joined the throng round the supper table and piled our plates with a delicious assortment of salads and quiches which Jayne and her Cordon-Bleu colleague Alice had made for the party.

'Keep me away from that basil butter, someone *please*.' Betty, who had a bit of a weight problem, was fighting her conscience over the baked potatoes.

'Hey Betty, come and squeeze in here.' I patted a vacant straw bale.

'Squeeze is the word. Why does that wretched girl have to be such a super cook?'

'Right,' I sympathised. 'Why don't you do what I do? Let yourself go over the savouries and go without cream on the fruit salad.'

'Good idea. Anyway, how are you both? And how's Hamish?'

'Fine. He's got ten wives now. I'm keeping them on the colony system for an experiment.' Betty, from fifteen years' rabbit keeping experience, pointed out a few drawbacks of the colony system, one of which was the amount of space it took up.

'I know,' I said. 'But we've decided to move. We've got too much house and too little land where we are.'

'M'm, you have. But what will you do for a living?'

'Well, according to my learned friend here' — I indicated Mandy, inelegantly tucking in to an acre of asparagus — 'I'm going to give riding lessons and Brian's going to grow things to sell. Flowers maybe. And we're going to keep more pigs.'

'I'll keep my ear to the ground for smallholdings for you,' Betty said.

'Thanks.' We took our plates back to the tables and wandered over to look at the raffle prizes displayed at the end of the barn. On a small table there were some pottery mugs, several pounds of butter and cream, bottled fruit, dried herbs and six fertile duck eggs. The floor space round the table was taken up with some fencing posts, a sack of potatoes, an unplucked chicken, two bales of hay and some blackcurrant bushes.

Mandy had implicit faith in my ability to 'influence' raffle tickets. She pressed her tickets into my hand and later, when the draw was made, wasn't nearly as surprised as I was when she got the prize of her choice — the six fertile duck eggs.

'*Magic*,' she said gleefully. 'I'll incubate them in the airing cupboard at home.'

'I wonder where smallholders keep their towels and pillow-cases,' someone said, and we all laughed. Warm cupboards were much too precious for linen. Where else could you put orphaned creatures, fermenting yogurt, rising bread or germinating seeds?

All too soon it was time to hand round coffee, then guide each others' cars safely out of the muddy farmyard. A super party we all agreed, and what a good idea to have it in a barn. Even a late arrival whose hands were criss-crossed with Elastoplast (she had been trying to pen a batch of aggressive drakes) had enjoyed it. She might have missed the food and the drink and the dancing but she hadn't been too late for Jayne's recipe for orange sauce.

*　　*　　*

Elizabeth came into season and was sent away to be mated to a young Hereford bull owned by Reg (the farmer who had had pneumonia) and his wife Polly who was an expert breeder.

The bull, a docile pipe-and-slippers sort of chap called Henry, was quietly pulling hay from his manger when Elizabeth was led in. The idea was to secure Elizabeth in the stall next to Henry's and let them get to know each other through the partition before getting down to the nitty gritty.

But Elizabeth had never seen a real bull before — her first husband had been the AI man — and she fell violently in love at first sight. So violently in fact that she reduced the wooden partition to splinters in her eagerness to get at him.

She reared up and brought her forelegs crashing down on the top rail, then heaved herself over the broken gap. Henry, who had had twenty-six other wives, went on eating his hay.

Elizabeth stayed with Henry for three days. He must have finished his hay because a month later the result of the pregnancy diagnosis was a triumphant 'positive'.

The cow herd then, was going to be increased by a hundred per cent. That meant another acre must be reserved for 'cattle' the following year. We pored over 'Smallholdings for Sale' columns in the local papers and tried to work out how much land would be needed for the stock we intended to carry in a year's time. One and a half cows, 7 pigs plus offspring, 5 ponies — maybe more if the riding lessons took off — 10 breeding does plus Hamish and all the poultry.

'Ten acres for the animals as a minimum,' Brian said, 'and a couple for hay — say fifteen acres to allow for, er, additions.' He said this with a hunted look, as though I was proposing to start breeding giraffes on any spare half acre.

'And what about us?' I said. 'Could we manage with a two up two down now that Marcus and Sara have gone?'

'They might come back,' Brian pointed out. I looked at him in dismay. We were on very good terms with both the children now that their noise and phone calls and complicated love lives were not under our roof, and had no desire to re-open hostilities. 'You don't really think they will, do you?'

No, he didn't, he was only pulling my leg. But talking of hostilities, wasn't it time to get the house on the market? And should we have estate agents?

Estate agents. A sub species on a par with tapeworms in our experience. We had moved eight times in twenty years and had met only one nice one in all that time. I don't know why we always delude ourselves that *this* time it will be different, this time we might find one who will actually sell the house.

We leafed through the papers and chose three agents whose adverts tended to be marginally less dishonest than the rest. At the same time we put our own ads in the *Sunday Times* and *Observer*.

'There's no call for these big places,' said agent number one. Brian and I looked at each other, and grinned. We had laid bets with each other as to which of the three would try that corny old gambit. The next bit would be a valuation thousands below the market price for a 'quick sale'. (The quick sale is to a crony of the agent. Then they resell the house at the right price and split the profit.)

'I think you should drop £8000,' continued the agent. 'For a quick sale.'

'We don't particularly want a quick sale,' said Brian mildly. 'We haven't a found a place to buy yet.'

'Oh.' The agent saw his month in St Tropez disappearing fast. He tried a different tack.

'It's a long way from anywhere, isn't it?'

We agreed that it was a long way from Oslo or Edinburgh but not a long way from fields of cowslips and wild orchids, bog plants and glow-worms.

When the printed particulars came we found to our surprise that far from being a long way from anywhere, the property was conveniently situated twixt Honiton and Taunton.

'Look at this Brian,' I giggled. '*Twixt.*'

'Let me switch on the "flourescant" light to get a better view of the most desirable sought after property,' said Brian. 'I see we're owners in residence, viewing by appt. only.'

The other two agents sent acned youths in well-cut dark suits to do battle. One saw it as a property offering unique opportunities for equestrian activity and the other a guest house easily converted to a Retirement Home, subject to the necessary planning permission. Viewing was by appt. only and *they* couldn't spell fluorescent either.

Meanwhile our *Sunday Times* advertisement had brought

twenty-eight replies, and of these six had made appointments to come and see us at the weekend. We polished the pigs, hosed away the chicken droppings in the yard and found the Rentokil survey report. (It was twixt the dog licences and an out-of-date passport.)

Brian showed the first four prospective buyers round on Saturday while I spent the day house hunting for ourselves. I took Mandy for company and the three of us compared notes in the evening.

'Two of mine were definitely interested,' Brian reported. 'An animal sanctuary and a woman with a million children. How did you get on?'

'Hopeless. Everything we saw was either too posh or too decrepit.'

'Too posh?' said Brian hopefully.

'Much too posh. You don't want to spend your life clipping hedges and shaving croquet lawns, do you?'

'Or putting a complete new roof on the place before you can live in it?' said Mandy. 'Different places,' she added, seeing his confused look. 'We saw seven and one didn't have a roof.'

We gave him a censored account of how we had collected a key to one empty house, let ourselves in and accidentally let four young bullocks in at the same time. We didn't know they had followed us. By the time we had finished exploring upstairs they had turned the scullery into a midden.

And another house, also empty because — as the agent put it — the owner had 'passed over'. It would have been all right if he had only said it once, but in some long rigmarole about executors, he kept saying it, and reduced Mandy and me to hysterics as we had visions of the old dear buzzing over the house like a low flying jet.

On the Sunday Brian went out viewing and I stayed at home to do the conducted tours. Neither of my customers found the place suitable (too small, said a would-be hotelier. Too big said a retired Army man with angina), but the caterer booked half a pig for Christmas, so the day wasn't wasted.

During the week Brian's people — the animal sanctuary and the woman with a million children — both made offers to buy at the asking price. Neither was caught up in a buying chain so it looked like a question of tossing for it. But then Mother Hubbard ruined her chances by offering to gazump by another five hundred pounds.

I was pleased it was going to be an animal sanctuary; I want one of my own someday when I can find a backer, so this seemed the next best thing. Brian blew the dust off the typewriter and was about to get the legal machinery in motion when a strange thing happened. The post came.

And in the post was a letter from Mr and Mrs Chambers, parents of Clare, Joe, Dan and Ant who had stayed with us for a week that summer. They — the parents — had been talking over the idea of buying a children's holiday farm themselves, and could we give them any tips?

'Tips?' said Brian, his eyes out on stalks as he read the letter. 'I think we can do a bit better than that.'

He screwed up his letter to our endlessly patient solicitor which began: 'Dear Geoffrey.' and started another: 'Dear Mr and Mrs Chambers, It just so happens. . .'

Chapter Twenty

WHILE WE WERE waiting for a reply from Mr and Mrs Chambers we stepped up the search for a smallholding for ourselves, acquiring in the process several more photographs to add to our collection of houses we didn't buy.

One of these was described in the agent's handout as Pair of Dwellings with Potential. It looked quite nice on the printed page and had fifteen acres and mains electricity. Why so cheap, we wondered, and went to find out.

The walls of Pair of Dwellings were all right as far as walls go. The drawback was that there were only three of them. We blinked and consulted the agent's particulars to make sure we had come to the right place. Yes, there was the photograph of the southern elevation and another one of the view from the back garden. But *nowhere* was there any mention of the fact that the entire northern side was shored up by massive girders and shrouded in a vast tarpaulin.

Brian, relieved to see that the tarpaulin was too soggy for me to chalk remarks on it, climbed back into the van and started the engine.

'Next stop the Quantocks,' he said, and off we went to view the ninth house in two days. Lovely it was too and reputedly once the home of Jane Austen. But it was too big. The rooms were so lofty we imagined that Jane Austen must have had to pen quite a few missives to the coalman before she could get stuck in to *Pride and Prejudice*. And so it went on. Everything seemed to be too big or too small, too trim and expensive or too derelict and deep in mud. House hunting in November is fine for seeing the faults in a place but you have to balance that against the tedium of constantly getting bogged down in muddy farmyards.

Concrete began to have an irresistible attraction and if we

managed to park on hard standing we would hear ourselves saying 'Haven't you got a lovely approach' to mystified farm owners who were all psyched up to show off their wall-to-wall Wilton.

There were verbal punch-ups with estate agents.

'Why can't you tell the *truth*?' Brian would snarl down the phone. 'Why didn't you say the place was a hovel? What? Yes it is, it's a hovel. Half the roof's missing and there's no lavatory. No, I don't call a hole in the ground half a mile from the back door a lavatory. Yes, I know I can get a council grant, but I'm not prepared to wait six months before I can have a pee. . .'

The more we saw, the more we didn't want to leave Phyllishayes. Not so much the house, which for all its charm would have made a super frog sanctuary in winter, but the holding itself; the cobbled yard and seven stables, the hay barn where young Don had devoured his Arthur Ransomes, the two garden areas which had given us hundredweights of vegetables and a never-ending supply of cut flowers, and, most of all, the view.

But as our ferretting friend Liz, had said, you can't eat the view.

John and Lin Chambers drove down from London with Clare, Joe, Dan and Ant and three-year-old Vicky who, after three months, was still miffed that the others had had a holiday without her.

'I'm coming to live in Pupottery,' she announced, as soon as she got out of the car. (We had heard Upottery called Uppity, Upover and You Pottery but Pupottery was a new one.)

'We all are,' said Ant.

'Quickest sale you're ever likely to make,' John laughed, shaking hands with Brian. Lin pretended it was hardly worth her getting out of the car as the children seemed quite capable of negotiating their own property deals.

The children ran off to show Vicky the ponies and their parents began a methodical tour of the house. Brian and I left them to it as there's nothing worse than having people breathing down your neck when you're trying to make up your mind.

Over lunch — homegrown pork and vegetables — we asked John and Lin why they wanted to leave London.

'For the same reasons as you two really,' Lin said. 'We want a slower pace of life.'

John worked in the City. His job sounded terribly demanding; a phone in each hand all day and decisions about foreign currency to be worked out at top speed. 'He's permanently tired,' Lin explained and giggled when Brian eyed the five children. 'Nearly always then,' she amended. 'Anyway we thought running a guest house would be a doddle for him after the Foreign Exchange. And it would be good for the kids to grow up in the country.'

Brian and I very much wanted them, rather than either of the other two prospective buyers, to have it because we liked them so much and because it would mean we wouldn't have to cancel next year's bookings. But we didn't want them to rush into the holiday business thinking it would be a rest cure.

'It's hard work,' we said. 'It's twenty-four hours a day, seven days a week. Lots of responsibility, lots of cooking and lots of noise.'

'A real home from home in other words,' John grinned.

'Yes, of course, you've had plenty of practice with your tribe I suppose. But somehow with twenty it's different. They egg each other on to do things they wouldn't do on their own.'

'Tell them about the Goat Show,' Brian suggested.

I shook my head. It was too soon after the event even to think about it let alone tell.

'We got thrown out,' Brian said simply. 'All twenty-four of us.'

Lin and John seemed satisfied with this distilled account and nodded understandingly.

'And then there was the night Elvis Presley died,' I remembered. 'The kids all went into a sort of mass hysteria.'

'I'm afraid I'd have no patience with anything like that,' Lin said. 'I'd have smacked their bottoms.'

'We did.' I said. 'Mary and Mandy and I smacked the lot of them. Trouble was they kept moving so some got smacked twice and some not at all. Still, at least they were crying for a reason afterwards.'

'Are we mad?' John said to Lin. 'Are we seriously thinking of taking on twenty hysterics a week?'

'It's not really as awful as we've been making out,' Brian laughed. 'We've been telling you the worst bits first. Would you like to see some slides of the holiday kids?'

'No,' they said firmly, and we didn't know them well enough to force them so we told them about Don and his books, and Quentin's plays and the Silver Jubilee fête.

And about the time an outraged six-year-old called Sonia started dragging all the blankets off her bed. 'What are you doing Sonia?' Mandy had asked.

'I'm taking my things into another bedroom. Mary said the vet's sleeping in this one. I don't like vets.'

'The vet?' Mandy said, puzzled. 'But we haven't called the vet. In any case he wouldn't be sleeping here, Sonia. Half a mo.' She called down the stairs. 'Hey Mary, what's this about the vet coming?'

'*Yvette*,' Mary corrected. 'I've put her in the small double with Sonia.'

'Oh Yvette. Of course.' Mandy turned to Sonia. 'It's a little girl Sonia, her name's Yvette.'

Don't be silly,' said Sonia. 'Nobody's called E. Vet.'

So many good memories. The odd mispronounced word or catch phrase would be with us long after we'd forgotten who started them. The record of Schubert's Trout could never be played now without remembering how someone had said 'Cod in batter is nicer.' Agricultural shows wouldn't be the same without twenty small companions loudly speculating on what was happening in the Breeding Pairs tent. And would we ever be able to watch the judging of animal exhibits again without doing what the kids always did – judge the handler not the animals? (Cor look, that ugly lady got a red rosette. What about that then?)

Happy times. Then I remembered the six hundred and two meals and Brian's frustration each time he found the kids or the pigs – or both – in among his pansies. No, it was time to move on.

✳   ✳   ✳

After lunch we toured the fields, proudly pointing out the drainage system which we had slaved over for a year and which now worked really well.

'When we came,' Brian explained, 'the water used to run off the fields and straight in at the front door. Now it's caught in this field drain' – he pointed to a brick-lined area under a hedge ' – and runs away underground.'

'Where does it run to?' Lin asked. A logical question and one which we couldn't answer. It seemed to us (and to many of our smallholding friends) that field drainage is like a sort of 'pass the parcel' game. Your field gets rained on and you've got to get rid of the surplus water before the music stops or you get flooded.

'It comes out lower down,' said Brian, dazzling us with his masterly grasp of physics.

'Well, that's a relief,' said John, winking at Lin. 'I don't like the sort that runs uphill.'

'But you have to keep it cleared of leaves and twigs,' Brian continued doggedly, 'and likewise stable drains.' Straight-faced he told them that stable drains have a calming effect on all other drains.

We stayed outside in the pale December sun, admiring the view and gymnastic display of the five children who were rediscovering the delights of five-bar gates.

'Oh bum.'

'Don't swear.'

'I'm not swearing.'

'You are.'

'Not.'

'Are.'

'Look stupid, bum doesn't count. Hey, Daddy, does bum count?'

'Count what?' said John.

'As swearing. Does bum count?'

John appeared to ponder. 'No,' he said gravely. 'No, bum doesn't count.'

'Can we have a dog when we move, Daddy, please?' asked Clare.

'Yes of course you can,' said John. The children hugged him

with excitement. Brian and I quite felt like hugging him ourselves. To have buyers who would take over the children's holiday project was lucky enough, but the fact that they were already thoroughly broken in to small children was a bonus.

'I'm going to call my dog Pupottery,' said Vicky.

She seemed to like the word. Lin said she had been driving the family mad since August talking about Pupottery. But this drip on a stone technique had evidently paid off.

'When were you thinking of moving?' John asked.

'Some time in the new year. Perhaps March. At any rate, when it's a bit warmer.'

That did it of course. Fate is not keen on people making their own arrangements and the very next property we went to view turned out to be a twenty acre smallholding so under-priced that we *had* to have it.

It wasn't really what we wanted. There were two snags: the first one was that even though it was underpriced it was too big and too expensive for us, and the second was that the vendor was caught up in a complicated buying chain and needed a quick sale. So quick in fact that Brian had to phone Geoffrey's practice in peak time to get the searches under way.

'My dear Brian,' said Geoffrey (he always says my dear Brian when he's exasperated), 'how the *hell* can you and Faith buy a Tudor farmhouse and twenty acres? You haven't got any money.'

'We will have when Phyllishayes is sold.'

'Phyllishayes *isn't* sold. It's not sold until I've seen a signed contract. And don't tell me your purchaser is a man of integrity because there's no such animal. Furthermore, if my arithmetic is correct you're still about twenty thou short for the Tudor pile.'

'Ah yes, I'm coming to that.' Brian lit a cigarette. 'You see the new house is quite big — not much smaller than Phyllishayes as a matter of fact — so Faith's mother is going to buy half and live there too.'

'Oh.' Geoffrey softened. He could see a glimmer of sanity about the new venture. 'She's sold her own house I take it?'

'Not yet,' Brian admitted.

'I see,' said Geoffrey with a sigh. 'You three want to buy a country estate. You haven't a bean between you. Right?'

'In a nutshell, Geoff.'

'And you want me to draw up a contract for the sale of Phyllishayes and see to a three-way purchase of the new place?'

'Right again, but it's got to be done in ten days because of the buying chain ahead of us.' He held the phone well away from his ear.

'*Ten days*? But it's *Christmas* in a fortnight.'

'You are still the fastest conveyancer in London, aren't you?'

'Yes I am. But I can't bloody well turn water into wine yet.'

Persuading Anne, my widowed mother, to move to the West Country had not been difficult. Moving house is commonplace in our family – once every two or three years is about the norm – and she jumped at the chance to renew her acquaintance with Pickfords.

Unfortunately for Pickfords her ideas on what constitutes normal household effects are somewhat eccentric. I blame the war. All that 'Don't Waste It' propaganda has stayed with quite a number of people of my mother's generation and they hoard string and jam jars and winkle out the last tealeaf in the packet as if the war was still going on. In Anne's case, this hoarding habit hadn't stopped at string and jam jars.

Sara and Gerry took a weekend off from their caretaking job to help Anne pack for the move. They were so staggered by the size of the task they didn't know where to start and phoned us for advice.

'What on earth was National Dried Milk?' Sara wanted to know. 'And does she really *need* thirty-two empty tins of it?'

'I'll tell you what we did before her last move,' I said. 'We bought a few dozen black bin bags and filled them two at a time so that she didn't notice. Then we dumped them at the council tip after dark.'

'Why didn't you take these National Dried Milk tins? Or the shedful of enamel pails?'

'We took the stuff in chronological order. We were still on stone ginger-beer bottles with a marble in the top last time. And 1920 knitting patterns for cloche hats.'

'Gerry reckons we've hit a 1945 seam. Ration books, gas masks, blackout material and radios that don't go — wirelesses Anne calls them — and plastic things that are too awful even for a jumble sale.'

'Bakelite.'

'What?'

'It's called Bakelite if it's pre-war. Plastic hadn't been invented.'

'Well, whatever it is it's horrible. And, by the way, the removal men won't take the hens or the poultry house.'

'No, I know. Brian will bring the Transit up for them on moving day. Any other problems?'

'Yes. She wants us to dig up Norman.'

'Dig up Norman? Hell, Sara, it's the middle of December. He might die of shock if he's woken up.'

'I know. But she insists. Says she can't leave him in case the new people don't give him his bread and milk when he wakes up.'

'OK. But leave him until moving day. Brian can dig him up at the last minute.'

Like not being a florist at Christmas, one of life's minor comforts is not being a clairvoyant. Had Brian foreseen a three hundred mile drive in freezing fog with twelve unconfined chickens and a mother-in-law who worried about the comfort of her two cats, two dogs and a hibernating hedgehog, he would never have set out so jauntily on that cold December morning.

Meanwhile there was our own move to attend to. Honey, a most conservative dog, took one look at the tea chests and withdrew to her basket, tail between legs. Great gusty sighs plainly saying 'Oh no *not* again' wafted out from under her blanket and we had to buy her a jumbo-size drum of dog choc drops before we could meet her reproachful brown eyes.

None of the other animals minded the growing piles of tea chests and books. In fact Small even tried to help by packing herself several times, and we had to be careful to check all containers in case she was under the contents. Tiggy, the outdoor cat, who'd been here when we arrived, was going to stay on as Phyllishayes' number one mouser, but everyone else was coming with us.

201

Easy, we thought — the new house was only ten miles away — we'll ferry most of the outdoor stuff over in the Transit, leaving the furniture and so forth for the removal men, and the farm animals for Tony's horse box.

Outdoor stuff is called 'deadstock' in farming circles, a misnomer if ever there was one. Rolls of pig netting, electric fencing, troughs and lengths of wood have very definite lives of their own. They grow upwards and sideways, mainly in the period between measuring them and trying to squeeze them in to the van. They grow again during the journey and perversely won't budge when you try to get them out again.

After a dozen or so ferrying trips we looked as though we'd done fifteen rounds with Henry Cooper, but the precious deadstock was safely stored under tarpaulins in a paddock at the new place and we felt confident that yet another move was going smoothly.

Next day the removal men arrived, admired the dogs and view, drank strong tea and said the sky looked threatening. They loaded all our things, drank some more tea and departed. Brian and I followed in our own van with the dogs and Small who mewed piteously all the way because she didn't like being in a cat basket.

The plan was for us to see to the unloading of the furniture, dispense more tea, then return to Phyllishayes to help Tony load the pigs (first trip), then the ponies, cow, rabbits and poultry in three more relays.

'Aren't the days getting short?' I remarked gaily to one of the removal men as we passed each other on the stairs. It really was remarkably dark for one o'clock; I could hardly find the phone that was ringing its head off in the unfamiliar hall.

'Hullo.' I do wish people wouldn't ring up to wish you happiness in your new home before you're even settled in.

'That you Faith?'

'Oh, hi Tony. We'll be over in a jiff. The men have nearly finished here. Have you started loading the pigs yet?'

'I've loaded them and I've unloaded them again.'

'Have you? Are they all right?'

Tony made the sort of noise that Brian makes when I'm being more than normally dim-witted. 'Of course they're all right. But I'm in trouble. My lorry's broken down.'

'*We're* in trouble,' I corrected. Visions of Rose Hip, Bramble and Briar plus their respective litters galloping along the road twixt Honiton and Taunton flashed through my mind. 'Is it serious Tony, the breakdown?'

'Aye. Fuel pump's gone. I've phoned the spares depot and they said I'll be lucky to get it repaired this side of Christmas.'

'What? Four days?'

'That's right. You'll have to come over twice a day to milk Elizabeth and feed them all. Lucky it's only ten miles, isn't it?'

I put the phone down and went outside to find Brian. Then it began to snow. . .

MRS BLAKE